THE
AFRICAN NATIONAL CONGRESS

SAUL DUBOW

JONATHAN BALL PUBLISHERS
JOHANNESBURG

Originally published in 2000 by
Sutton Publishing Ltd
England

This edition published in 2000 by
Jonathan Ball Publishers (Pty) Ltd
P O Box 33977
Jeppestown
2043

ISBN 1-86842-097-3

Cover photographs by courtesy of *The Sunday Times*.

Typeset in 11/13 pt Baskerville.
Typesetting and origination by
Sutton Publishing Limited.
Printed in Great Britain by
Cox & Wyman, Reading, Berkshire.

Contents

Map		iv
List of Dates		v
Preface		x
Introduction		xii
1.	Beginnings	1
2.	Protest or Resistance	8
3.	Renewal and Radicalisation	20
4.	Civil Disobedience and Defiance	34
5.	The Congress of the People and the Freedom Charter	46
6.	Towards Sharpeville	59
7.	The Struggle Moves Underground	66
8.	A Revival in Internal Opposition	79
9.	The Revolt of the 1980s	84
10.	Negotiations	95
	Conclusion	102
	Further Reading	111
	Index	114

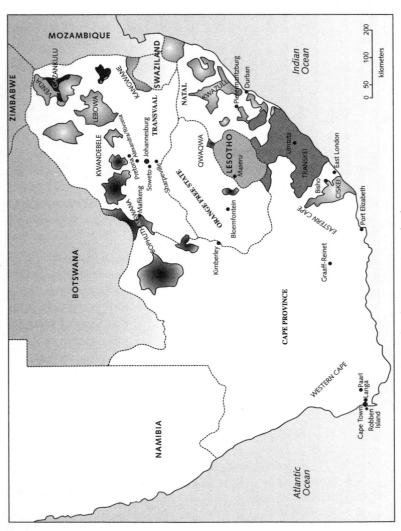

South Africa, c. 1985, showing provinces and Bantustan/Homelands.

List of Dates

1899–1902 South African or Anglo–Boer War

1902 Foundation of African People's Organisation (Cape Town); M.K. Gandhi establishes *Indian Opinion* newspaper

1906 Bambatha rebellion (Zululand)

1910 Union of South Africa; Louis Botha becomes first South African prime minister

1912 Formation of South African Native National Congress (later ANC)

1913 Natives' Land Act; Orange Free State women's anti-pass campaign; Indian passive resistance campaign

1914 Formation of National Party under Hertzog; South Africa enters war on Allied side; Afrikaner rebellion crushed; SANNC deputation goes to London

1916 Publication of Solomon Plaatje's *Native Life in South Africa*

1918 African sanitary workers strike in Johannesburg

1919 Foundation of Industrial and Commercial Workers' Union; Smuts succeeds Louis Botha as prime minister; SANNC deputation to Versailles; SANNC-led anti-pass demonstrations

1920 African mineworkers strike, Johannesburg

1921 Bulhoek Massacre; formation of Communist Party of South Africa

1922 Rand Revolt; Bondelswarts rebellion crushed

1923 Natives (Urban Areas) Act; renaming of SANNC as ANC

1924 National Party under Hertzog wins election in coalition with Labour; Z.R. Mahabane becomes ANC president

1926 Hertzog's Segregation Bills first tabled

1927	Native Adminstration Act; Josiah Gumede becomes president of ANC
1928	Adoption of 'native republic' policy by Communist Party
1930	Pixley Seme replaces Josiah Gumede as ANC president
1934	Hertzog and Smuts form South African (National) Party; Malan forms (Purified) National Party
1935	Formation of All-African Convention
1936	Passage of Hertzog's Segregation Bills through parliament
1939	Smuts becomes prime minister when South Africa enters war on Allied side
1940	Alfred Xuma becomes ANC president
1941	Formation of African Mineworkers' Union
1943	*African Claims* adopted by ANC; Alexandra bus boycott
1944	Formation of ANC Youth League; Alexandra bus boycott
1946	African Mineworkers' Strike; adjournment of Natives' Representative Council
1947	'Doctor's Pact' between ANC and Indian Congress leaders
1948	National Party under Malan comes to power
1949	ANC adopts Programme of Action; Cato Manor riots; James Moroka succeeds Xuma as ANC president
1950	Population Registration, Group Areas, Suppression of Communism Acts; dissolution of Communist Party; National Day of Protest and Mourning; Witzieshoek uprising
1951	Bantu Authorities Act
1952	Defiance Campaign launched; Luthuli succeeds Moroka as ANC president
1953	Bantu Education, Criminal Law Amendment, Public Safety Acts; formation of Coloured People's Organisation, Congress of Democrats and Liberal Party
1954	Formation of Federation of South African Women

LIST OF DATES

1954–5	Destruction of Sophiatown
1955	Congress of the People at Kliptown adopts Freedom Charter; formation of Congress of South African Trade Unions
1956	Removal of Coloureds from common voters' roll; Women's march to Pretoria
1956–61	Treason Trial
1957	Rural disturbances in Sekhukuneland, Zeerust, Pondoland
1958	Verwoerd becomes prime minister
1959	Formation of Pan-Africanist Congress; Promotion of Bantu Self-Government act
1960	Sharpeville massacre and Langa disturbances; State of emergency imposed; banning of ANC, PAC and Communist Party; Pondoland Revolt; Oliver Tambo establishes ANC in exile
1961	Umkhonto we Sizwe (ANC military wing) launches guerrilla action; South Africa leaves Commonwealth and becomes a republic
1962	Mandela tours Africa and Britain and is later arrested; United Nations votes for sanctions against South Africa
1963	'90 Day Act'; arrest of Umkhonto leaders at Rivonia
1964	Mandela, Sisulu and Rivonia leadership sentenced to life imprisonment
1966	Verwoerd assassinated. John Vorster becomes prime minister
1967	Oliver Tambo becomes acting ANC president-general on death of Luthuli
1969	ANC Morogoro conference, Tanzania; formation of South African Students's Association
1971	Re-launch of Natal Indian Congress
1972	Formation of Black People's Convention
1973	Durban Strikes

1975	Formation of Inkatha movement under Buthelezi; independence of Mozambique and Angola
1976	Soweto Uprising; Transkei first homeland to gain 'independence'
1977	Killing of Steve Biko in police detention; banning of Black Consciousness organisations
1978	P.W. Botha replaces Vorster as prime minister; death of Sobukwe
1979	Formation of Azanian People's Organisation and Congress of South African Students; Riekert and Wiehahn commissions propose trade union and urban reforms
1980	School boycotts; Zimbabwe gains independence; Umkhonto sabotage of SASOL refinery
1982	Conservative Party breaks away from governing party; Umkhonto attack on Koeberg nuclear power station
1983	Formation of United Democratic Front and National Forum; adoption of new constitution
1984	Elections for tri-cameral parliament; start of Vaal Uprising
1985	Formation of Congress of South African Trade Unions; violence intensifies; killings at Langa on 25th anniversary of Sharpeville; selective state of emergency imposed; Botha delivers 'Rubicon' speech; disinvestment campaign gathers pace
1986	Largest ever national stay-away; imposition of nationwide state of emergency; US Congress passes Comprehensive Anti-Apartheid Act; abolition of pass laws; military raids on ANC bases in neighbouring countries as Commonwealth Eminent Persons Group attempts negotiations
1987	Oliver Tambo meets US Secretary of State; white opinion-formers meet with ANC in Dakar; National Union of Mineworkers strike; release of Govan Mbeki;

	Inkatha/UDF violence escalates in Natal
1988	UDF affiliates suppressed; agreement of terms of Namibian independence agreed; efforts to broker peace in Natal conflict fail
1989	F.W. de Klerk succeeds P.W. Botha as leader of National Party and later as president; Mandela meanwhile meets Botha; Sisulu and others released from prison
1990	Unbanning of ANC, PAC and Communist Party. Release of Mandela, who becomes de facto leader of the ANC; Namibia gains independence; formal talks begin between ANC and government; state of emergency lifted; violence between Inkatha and ANC/UDF supporters spreads to Witwatersrand
1991	Convention for a Democratic South Africa (Codesa) meets to negotiate new constitution; repeal of key apartheid legislation; Mandela and Buthelezi meet in unsuccessful attempt to contain Inkatha–ANC violence; UDF dissolves; Mandela elected president of ANC with Tambo as chairman and Cyril Ramphosa as secretary-general; ANC announces campaign of mass action
1992	Launch of Patriotic Front of all anti-apartheid organisations; Inkatha refuses to attend second session of Codesa; intensification of violence between ANC and Inkatha; suspension of Codesa talks after Boipatong massacre; informal talks between government and ANC continue; Record of Understanding signed between ANC and government
1993	Formal negotiations resume between 26 parties; Chris Hani assassinated; date for elections set for 27 April 1994; Mandela and de Klerk jointly win Nobel Peace Prize; transitional constitution agreed
1994	ANC wins first non-racial democratic elections; Government of National Unity formed with Mandela as president

ix

Preface

As a historian of modern South Africa, but not one who has specialised in the history of resistance politics, Asa Briggs' invitation to write a short history of the African National Congress provided a welcome opportunity to make comprehensible a complex story for myself and, hopefully, others as well. The task proved even more difficult than originally anticipated. Writing a condensed history in a manner that should be accessible to a putative 'general audience', while also being acceptable to experts, is a difficult challenge. Nor has it been easy to write a balanced history of a controversial and politically sensitive movement in a country whose past is even more difficult to explain than its future is to predict. My own interpretive inclinations – which stress the contingencies of historical outcomes and are sceptical of nationalist teleologies – are to some extent at odds with my contracted task: to write an institutionally focused history of the ANC from its foundation in 1912 to its accession to power in 1994. A broader and deeper study of the history of liberation movements in South Africa would have to take far greater account of the multiplicity and complexity of oppositional struggles than I have been able to do. It would also be more sensitive to the rhythms of local political traditions, the intricacies of dissident political cultures, and the social historian's 'view from below'. This said, it is somewhat surprising that no reliable, unpartisan and well-researched general history of the ANC from its foundation to the present exists. Institutional histories tell only part of the story, but a vital part none the less.

Peter Vale, Paul la Hausse and Mark Gevisser have all commented critically on aspects of the draft text. Without necessarily agreeing with my conclusions – or even agreeing among themselves – they have spared me errors and have alerted me to omissions and pitfalls. I owe them profound thanks.

Introduction

Nelson Mandela was finally released from incarceration on 11 February 1990, nearly three decades after being sentenced to life imprisonment for crimes of treason committed against the apartheid state. Emerging slowly through the gates of Paarl's Victor Verster prison into the brilliant Cape summer sunshine, his short and hesitant walk to freedom was witnessed by a global television audience of hundreds of millions. Mandela was, at the age of seventy-one, a living embodiment of the human struggle for freedom, a leader of iconic status who enjoyed unequalled moral stature within the liberation movement. But in many respects he was still an unknown quantity. Had Mandela been quietly released from prison he would probably not even have been publicly recognised because the only photographs that existed of him were a quarter of a century old. Forbidden to communicate directly with the outside world, most of Mandela's political views had to be gleaned through intermediaries or inferred. Thus, the enigma of the man, the mythology that surrounded him, and the euphoria of the moment only served to heighten public expectancy. Notwithstanding the palpable aura of greatness that surrounded him, some observers found themselves wondering whether Mandela could possibly live up to the expectations that the world had of him. At his advanced age and with his state of health an unknown factor, would Mandela be able to resume an effective public role? Was he merely a figurehead leader who would easily be subject to manipulation by secret cabals? Alternatively, might he act on his own initiative without due consultation, renege on the ANC's putative socialist principles, and unilaterally suspend the armed struggle? Most important, could Mandela and the ANC finally wrest power from a minority government that was evidently still very much in control?

In the light of Mandela's extraordinary statesmanship and his unique role in bringing a spirit of reconciliation to a country on the brink of anarchy and civil war, it is instructive to recall some of the doubts and fears that surrounded him at the time of his release. History is apt to confer a retrospective sense of certainty and inevitability on the past, and to occlude the role of contingency and fortune in events. Thus, it is important to remember that, for a great deal of his long stretch on Robben Island, Mandela was virtually forgotten by the world; he might easily have died a prisoner along with others of his close compatriots had the so-called 'South African miracle' not taken the form that it did.

The accession to power of the ANC in 1994 confirmed in many minds the sense that its victory had been historically ordained. The ANC itself has been keen to encourage this view, not least because it helps to legitimise its claim to be the natural custodian of liberation and freedom. Several accounts of the ANC have written its story in terms of successes and reverses, lessons learned, mistakes repaired. But there was no automatic progression and no certainty as regards the eventual outcome of the struggle. As the oldest and most enduring political organisation on the African continent, the ANC always maintained a special place in the nationalist movement. But on several occasions in its long history the ANC's paramount position was rivalled by other political organisations; there were long periods during which it was effectively moribund; sometimes it was more of an onlooker than an active participant in events; often it was accused by its own supporters of pusillanimity. That the majority of South Africans would eventually secure their freedom was a widely and long-held view, both within and outside the country. But this was partly a matter of faith. The wry joke that liberation would come within five years – only no one knew when to start counting – was almost as true in the mid-1980s as it had been in the early 1960s.

ONE

Beginnings

In January 1912 a large gathering of prominent African men and women met in Bloemfontein to form the South African Native National Congress. The principal purpose of this new organisation (which changed its name to the African National Congress a decade later) was to defend and advance African civil and political rights at a time when these were under unprecedented threat. Two years earlier the Union of South Africa had been constituted, signalling the emergence for the first time of a unitary white supremacist state. Union was achieved in the wake of the traumatic Anglo–Boer War (1899–1902) which led to British authority in the colonies of the Cape and Natal finally being extended over the previously independent Boer republics of the Transvaal and the Orange Free State. The war bore many of the hallmarks of a civil conflict and, although it represented a crushing defeat for Afrikaners in the short term, the long-term losers were Africans whose interests were sacrificed in the pursuit of white unity and reconciliation. In the years after 1910 blacks' political rights and economic security came under sustained attack. Although Africans and Coloureds in the Cape retained important residual political rights – most importantly, the possibility of qualifying for the common franchise – these privileges were denied to their compatriots in the other three provinces of the new South Africa. Under the banner of racial segregation concerted moves were made to restrict African landownership rights and to compel the majority of African peasant cultivators to become wage labourers for white farmers and industrialists.

The SANNC was by no means the first organisation dedicated to representing the interests of non-white South Africans. As early as the 1880s élite Africans had formed political groupings and newspapers to voice their concerns. Other 'non-white' groups were also active from an early date: for example, the Natal Indian Congress, founded in 1894 (which may well be the source of the term 'Congress' in South Africa), and the 'Coloured' African People's Organisation, formed in 1902. The distinctiveness of the SANNC lies in the fact that it was the first political organisation to be constituted on a genuinely national rather than a regional basis – as the words 'South African' in its original title clearly indicates. In line with its nationalist

2

objectives the SANNC was therefore dedicated to overcoming inter-African ethnic divisions and to extending citizenship and franchise rights to all South Africans on a non-racial basis.

The SANNC's leadership was predominantly drawn from those aspirant members of the African proto-middle classes – doctors, lawyers, ministers, landowners and traders – who stood to lose most from the post-Union political dispensation. John Dube, the SANNC's founder president, was an American-trained Zulu educationist, minister and newspaper editor who was deeply influenced by Booker T. Washington's moderate advocacy of racial coexistence and Negro self-sufficiency; its secretary, Solomon Plaatje, was a newspaper editor and author whose many literary accomplishments include his novel *Mhudi* and his translations of Shakespeare into Setswana; Pixley ka Izaka Seme, its treasurer, was a young lawyer trained at Columbia, Oxford and London, whose early leanings towards pan-Africanism suggest an acquaintance with the ideas of the leading black American thinker W.E.B. Du Bois. Other influential founder members such as Alfred Mangena and Richard Msimang were lawyers too.

In a gesture towards rural traditions and in recognition of their status and support base, prominent chiefs were accorded honorary positions within the SANNC hierarchy. However, the SANNC's leading figures were invariably drawn from the *kholwa*, a Zulu word denoting Christian converts. Typically, these professional men – and occasionally women – extolled Victorian values of moral improvement, material progress and personal respectability. Photographs of the Congress leadership reveal them posed in formal suits and hats, a dress code that neatly reflects their modernising ambitions as well as their social conservatism. Senior Congress figures, often members of the small and closely interconnected African bourgeoisie, were typically products of the network of mission schools which were established in the countryside and towns of South Africa from the mid-nineteenth century onwards. A number had subsequently gone on to study abroad in England, Scotland or the United States. Their hopes for inclusion within the South African body politic as citizens of a common, non-racial society were strongly informed by Christian and liberal conceptions of justice and humanity. While proud of their African identity, they eagerly embraced the universal qualities of Western civilisation in the belief that its principles were colour-blind and potentially of value to all.

The attitudes and social aspirations of many early African nationalist leaders were attuned to an optimistic age of improvement and liberal reform, but the political strategies born of such hopes proved unpropitious at a time of deepening racial and social division. In the first decade of the SANNC's existence the fledgling organisation was forced onto the defensive as the South African state consolidated its power and pressed for more and more regulatory control over the black population. The first major challenge faced by the SANNC after the Act of Union and the introduction of discriminatory labour legislation in 1911 was the passage of the 1913 Natives Land Act. Under the provisions of this measure thousands of African labour-tenants were expelled from white farms, especially in the Orange Free State, and just over 7 per cent of the country's land mass was apportioned to two-thirds of its population. The Act was applied neither comprehensively nor systematically and it contained a promise to extend the area reserved for African usage in time. Although the precise nature of future policy was uncertain, it was apparent that segregationist forces were hardening. In *Native Life in South Africa* (London, 1916; Harlow, 1987), a moving elegy to the evictions of individual African sharecroppers and labour tenants from white-owned farms, Sol Plaatje captured the Land Act's symbolic meaning in a phrase that continues to haunt South African historical memory: 'Awaking on Friday morning, June 20, 1913 the South African native found himself, not actually a slave, but a pariah in the land of his birth.' (1987 edn, p. 6)

Plaatje wrote these words on his way to Britain as part of a SANNC delegation which attempted unsuccessfully to lobby official and public opinion against the South African government. Deputations, petitions and reasoned argument were the preferred tactics adopted by Congressmen at this stage (a partial exception being the women's anti-pass campaigns of 1913–14 and 1919 which prompted Charlotte Maxeke to establish a Bantu Women's League under the aegis of the SANNC). In 1914 and again in 1919 delegations sailed to England. Here SANNC representatives protested against the Land Act, emphasised the loyalty displayed by blacks to the British cause during the South African and the First World Wars, and reminded the King of his obligations to uphold colour-blind principles throughout the Empire. The appeals of the SANNC leadership were couched in the language of duty and obligation, and they readily paid obeisance to an idealised notion of British fair play and justice. But although these deputations gained the support of some liberal groupings and were granted audiences by senior political leaders like Lloyd George, they were generally ignored by the imperial governing classes whose primary concern remained focused on maintaining good relations with the Afrikaner leaders of their former colony.

Reflecting on this period of protest, later generations of political activists and scholars have sometimes been dismissive of the ANC's early leadership, criticising it as overly deferential, naïve, and élitist. Congress's leaders were undoubtedly committed to a form of opposition which stressed responsible citizenship and disdained popular agitation. The impact of Congress was weakened by political inexperience, internal divisions, and, in some cases, a willingness to accept the principle of segregation so long as a fairer distribution of land could be secured. It is easy to judge the SANNC harshly for its willingness to compromise, its lack of militancy, and its unquestioning commitment to constitutionalism. But to do so is to ignore the fact that the full implications of segregation were not yet clear. Direct opposition to colonial oppression was no longer an option after the crushing of the 1906 Bambatha rebellion in Zululand. Africans, who had invested so much in becoming exemplary middle-class citizens of the British Empire, could not be expected to abandon their hard-won privileges without protest. In reminding the King and his government of the mutual obligations enshrined in the imperial 'civilising mission', Africans were therefore not simply engaged in acts of colonial mimicry; they were asserting and affirming their identities and rights as British subjects and confirming their deeply held liberal beliefs. The resort to moral suasion was a pragmatic strategy that had to be exhausted before being abandoned – as it largely was after 1919.

TWO

Protest or Resistance

In this initial phase of political mobilisation Congress was conspicuously ineffective in so far as reversing the provisions of the Land and Union Acts was concerned. However, the SANNC could take comfort from the fact that it had successfully positioned itself as the leading voice of African opinion with solid credentials as a broad-based centrist organisation committed to the eradication of racial prejudice and the promotion of human dignity. These values represented the basis of an enduring liberal-minded political tradition whose core components mixed appeals to moral authority with a measure of pragmatism and a willingness to compromise. As an umbrella organisation, Congress maintained strong links with the old chiefly aristocracy while nevertheless remaining vigorously opposed to tribalism and ethnic particularism. The form of nationalism it espoused was inclusive and expansive, while its strong Christian ethos remained universalist and ecumenical. In passing, it may be observed that the incorporative religious and nationalist traditions of Congress contrasted with the exclusivist strains of Christian Nationalism that were beginning to find a strong voice in Afrikaner political circles.

Increasing social and political pressures during the 1920s exposed the contradictions, tensions and organisational inadequacies of the early SANNC. The First World War was a vital catalyst of social change and, as happened elsewhere in the world, it served to stimulate nationalist awareness and anti-colonial resistance in many parts of Africa. The South African economy expanded rapidly during and immediately after the war, but this short boom was soon arrested by a sharp recession which set in from 1920. The postwar decade was marked by an unprecedented degree of social conflict affecting rural as well as urban areas. This was in itself testimony to the growing economic integration of industrial South Africa and the increasing centrality of the migrant labour system in the diamond and gold-mining economy which developed around Kimberley and Johannesburg from the 1870s. Segregation was intended to control the process of African urbanisation by enforcing racially based spatial, social and political distinctions wherever feasible. But the assumption of a dual rural/urban economy upon which this conception rested was mistaken; whites and blacks were mutually interdependent, and political separation could only be achieved by privileging one group at the expense of another.

Symptomatic of South Africa's growing economic integration – and social division – was the postwar upsurge in industrial action. Strikes, which had hitherto been largely restricted to white workers, were now taken up by blacks too, although the racial and structural barriers between them meant that the prospect of white and black workers acting in unison was remote. In 1918 a strike by African sanitary workers in Johannesburg seeking improved pay and protesting against the hated pass laws (which restricted Africans' residential rights and geographical mobility) provoked sympathy action on the part of black miners; in 1919 the Transvaal section of Congress organised a campaign of passive resistance against the pass laws; in the same year the Industrial and Commercial Workers Union was formed at the Cape Town docks by the charismatic and mercurial Clements Kadalie; in 1920 there was a major strike on the Witwatersrand gold-mines involving more than half of the entire black workforce; the following year police killed more than 180 members of the Israelites, an independent Christian African sect which had occupied land in the rural eastern Cape while awaiting its leader's prophecy of delivery from oppression. The secretary of the Native Affairs Department noted ruefully in his annual report for 1919–21 that the 'inevitable development of race-consciousness has begun and is showing itself in the formation of associations for all kinds of purposes – religious, political, industrial and social'.

The African National Congress played a secondary role in the social ferment of the 1920s and found itself partially eclipsed by other more radical movements and organisations. In the countryside a combination of drought, crop failure and increasing land hunger provided fertile ground for social unrest. Separatist dreams of a world free of white influence represented one sort of response to the growing rural crisis – a mirror, in some respects, of segregationist thinking. A millenarian movement led by Wellington Butelezi reinvigorated long-standing traditions of resistance to colonial encroachment by calling on Africans to stop paying taxes and to suspend cattle dipping. The growing influence of the transatlantic connection could be seen in Butelezi's appeal to the radical black liberationalist faith proclaimed by the Jamaican-born American, Marcus Garvey, whose powerful pan-Africanist dream of an 'Africa for the Africans' was eagerly taken up in some of the most remote parts of South Africa at this time. Butelezi promised that African-Americans would arrive in aeroplanes and deliver his followers from oppression. Garveyite ideas were also evident in the Industrial and Commercial Workers' Union, which grew to become the most powerful organ of black protest in the 1920s. Although founded as a trade union, the ICU discovered its real heartland among agricultural labourers in the countryside and rapidly established itself in Natal and the Transvaal. Issuing farmworkers with red membership cards and promising them protection from harsh employers, the ICU's initials were rendered into a powerful warning: 'I see you, white man.'

In the urban areas the Communist Party of South Africa (CPSA), formed in 1921, provided a new focus for socialist aspirations. Although the Russian Revolution provided it with the force of historic precedent and liberatory promise, the CPSA was by no means free of racist assumptions and was deeply divided between those adherents who identified the white working classes as the likeliest source of revolutionary action and others who recognised that blacks constituted the majority of the proletariat. These divisions were brought into dramatic focus during the 1922 Rand Revolt, when a strike by white mineworkers protesting against the erosion of the industrial job colour bar sparked an insurrection in Johannesburg which the Smuts government was only able to put down by bringing in the troops and bombarding strikers from the air. The bloody defeat of the white mineworkers was followed by the electoral victory in 1924 of J.B.M. Hertzog's National Party, which had entered into a somewhat unlikely class alliance with the largely English-speaking Labour

Party. The result was the political incorporation of white labour into the state and ever greater stratification of the working class along lines of colour.

Recognising these developments, the Communist Party began actively to recruit African support and by 1928 the great majority of its 1,750 members were blacks. Links were also forged with the ICU, which reached the peak of its influence in the late 1920s but thereafter went into rapid decline. In 1927 James la Guma travelled to Moscow as a representative of the CPSA, together with Josiah Gumede, the new president of the ANC. Gumede had been strongly influenced by Garveyite ideas and pronounced himself highly impressed by what he saw of the Bolshevik Revolution. The Gumede-La Guma trip inaugurated a relationship between the ANC and the CPSA which has endured in one form or another ever since. This association was cemented when the CPSA, in 1928, defined its principal objective as the fight for an 'independent native republic'.

The 'native republic' declaration acknowledged that South Africa was not yet ripe for revolution and that, as a 'British dominion of a colonial type', it was necessary to secure a bourgeois nationalist revolution before socialism could be achieved. In subsequent years this position was revised, elaborated and redefined, but the presumption of a two-stage revolution remained an article of faith for the Communist Party. Although this formulation drew to some extent on local experience of peasant insurrection and reflected the Party's growing Africanisation, it was in fact decreed by the Comintern. The 'native republic' policy offered considerable potential to create an alliance between nationalist and socialist forces, but it was deeply resented by those who felt that communism's class-based objectives had been diluted. Implementation of the policy proved highly debilitating. Recriminations and purges split the Party into competing factions, and the CPSA ceased to exist as an effective force during the 1930s.

The ANC was also fragmented and divided during the 1930s. In Natal and the Western Cape it split into competing factions reflecting ideological divisions, personal rivalries and tensions between the national leadership and local currents of popular opinion. The failures of its initial phase of respectful protest meant that the ANC was mostly unable or unwilling to engage with the spirit of postwar social radicalism that swept the country. There are important exceptions to this generalisation. In the Transvaal, for example, postwar industrial unrest had radicalised some of the ANC intelligentsia, who became alerted to the importance of securing a mass support base among the growing black proletariat. Paralleling this growing militancy, albeit in a different ideological key, Elliot Tonjeni and Bransby Ndobe cultivated a populist constituency in the Western Cape from the mid-1920s by attacking the ANC's susceptibility to white paternalism and proclaiming Garveyite-inflected nostrums instead. This eclectic infusion of popular radicalism was considerably influenced by the successes of the ICU and the Communist Party, whose political programmes were directly geared towards confronting the harshening segregationist climate and exploiting Africans' increasing impatience with conventional methods of protest.

The presence from the 1920s of Communist and Africanist groupings within the ANC was to be of considerable long-term significance for the organisation. Under different guises and at varying times, the core philosophies they represented were to emerge and re-emerge as ongoing political traditions. For the most part, as political logic would suggest, socialists and Africanists situated themselves at polar ends of the ANC and pulled the organisation in opposing directions: the former stressed non-racialism and class solidarity; the latter emphasised African self-sufficiency and the primacy of ethnic or racial struggle. However, as we shall see, at key historical moments the two traditions coalesced to produce a composite form of indigenous radicalism embodied in the vague but often compelling idea of African socialism. When contained by powerful centrist forces, such forms of militancy provided Congress with added dynamism and popular appeal; but in the absence of a constraining political environment, serious potential for instability existed within the organisation.

In the late 1920s and 1930s Congress leaders proved unable to contain and direct the radical possibilities offered by Africanism and socialism. For a brief moment the potential was there when Josiah Gumede – who displayed elements of Africanist as well as Marxist influence – was elected president-general of the ANC in 1927. In April 1930, however, he was deposed by Pixley Seme, who now stood as a representative of the ANC's moderate old guard. Seme's election took place in the context of a vituperative meeting during which radicals accused moderates of displaying timid resistance to Hertzog's segregationist measures, of being far too dependent on the support of liberal white intermediaries, and of being the tools of capitalist interests. For its part, the senior ANC establishment was suspicious of the influence of the Communist Party, resentful of militant attacks on Christian beliefs, and defensive about its restrained and orderly conduct in opposing segregation. Gumede's defeat was followed by an attempt by radicals in the Western Cape to inaugurate a campaign of civil disobedience in pursuit of the 'black republic'. But it was weakened by internal factional divisions which led to the creation of a short-lived left-wing 'Independent ANC' after the expulsion of Tonjeni and Ndobe from the parent body. In Natal, too, ANC politics became highly divisive by virtue of a split between Gumede and Dube, a situation that was further complicated by the presence of George Champion, who pursued his own political agenda as leader of a break-away segment of the ICU. These fissiparous regional forces, coinciding to a considerable degree with language differences and ethnic rivalries, further undermined the authority of the ANC national executive. As a result, the precipitous decline in ANC branch membership and activity continued.

If the ANC had been outflanked by radical impulses in the 1920s and proved unable to project itself as a focus of unified African political resistance, its record in the 1930s was even less successful. The virtual disappearance of the ICU and the Communist Party created a political vacuum. Seme's 1930 leadership team was dominated by ANC veterans who were ill suited to revive the organisation's fortunes and brought with them old men's squabbles and jealousies. Not for the last time in its history generational conflict and patronage politics were evident in internal Congress struggles; but instead of the senior establishment acting as a steadying influence – as it was largely able to do in the 1940s – the ANC leadership split into warring cliques.

The fight against segregation reached a peak in 1936 with the legislative enactment of Hertzog's land and franchise bills. Here the ANC was only one protesting organisation among several and although Congress rejected discriminatory policies, it did so only in a reactive and defensive manner. The ANC remained trapped within a segregationist discourse of compromise and concession which determined that the loss of franchise and citizenship rights enjoyed by a minority of Africans should be set against improvements in the amount of land apportioned for the use of the majority. Continued participation by ANC representatives in white-dominated welfare and lobbying organisations (like the Joint Councils of Europeans and Natives) had the effect of blunting vigorous opposition to the overall direction of government policy.

By the mid-1930s the ANC was weaker than it had ever been. Although the statistics are highly unreliable and require interpretation, it is probable that country-wide membership was not much in excess of 1,000 at this time, compared with 3–4,000 in the Cape and Transvaal alone during the early 1920s. Opposition to the final stages of Hertzog's 'Native Bills' was led not by the ANC but by a specially constituted organisation, the All-African Convention. Its president, D.D.T. Jabavu, was a respected academic and liberal politician who personified the political and social aspirations of the nineteenth-century Cape African élite. Co-operation between the ANC and the All-African Convention was facilitated by the fact that the two organisations shared a similar political outlook and support base. There was indeed a marked degree of convergence at leadership levels between them, but

Jabavu was not himself an ANC member, and Seme was not well disposed towards the Convention.

Paradoxically, the ANC's weakness compared to the Convention during the mid-1930s may ultimately have worked to its advantage, because the Convention was tainted by its involvement in a last-minute political compromise with the government on the issue of Hertzog's Native Bills in 1935–6 Jabavu in particular was blamed for conceding the principle of the African franchise and, although the Convention took a more radical turn in the 1940s under the influence of a grouping of Coloured Trotskyites and independent socialists based in the western Cape, it was seen to have failed in its principal declared purpose of resisting segregation. By contrast, the moribund ANC was spared direct criticism. The conspicuous failure of the politics of negotiation opened up the political landscape and prompted the beginnings of a process of intellectual and organisational renewal within the organisation. This began in 1936 when Seme was replaced as president-general by Revd James Calata, who was in turn succeeded by Z.R. Mahabane in 1938. A number of energetic young thinkers joined the ANC at this time, including R.H. Godlo, Z.K. Matthews, J.B. Marks, Edwin Mofutsanyana, H. Nkadimeng and Govan Mbeki. Their arrival did much to reinvigorate the ANC over the next decade.

19

THREE

Renewal and Radicalisation

The process of rebuilding Congress was accelerated when Dr Alfred B. Xuma took over its leadership in 1940 at the relatively young age of forty-seven. A former vice-president of the All-African Convention, Xuma had received extensive training as a medical doctor in the United States and Europe. With his high personal standing, Xuma was well placed to act as a transitional figure between the old ANC élite and the new mass politics of the 1940s centred on the industrial Transvaal. Xuma's greatest achievement was to rebuild the organisational structures of Congress. During his tenure the Congress branch structure was revived and expanded; membership increased considerably (it was around 4,000 in 1945); there was some alleviation in the chronically poor financial situtation; the non-functional upper House of Chiefs was formally abolished; women were accorded full membership rights, and a youth wing was established.

The 1940s was not only a formative period in the history of the ANC and African nationalism; it also provided a powerful impetus to extreme Afrikaner nationalism. A decade that began with the country's entry into the Second World War under the leadership of General Smuts concluded with the victory of D.F. Malan's National Party in 1948 and the official inauguration of apartheid. African politics were also deeply affected by the war experience. Rapid industrial growth, particularly in the manufacturing sector, drew massive numbers of black work-seekers into the major cities. A lack of adequate facilities and housing gave rise to a profusion of informal settlements and stimulated the growth of huge squatter encampments in urban areas adjoining Johannesburg and Durban. Many of these new arrivals were families from the increasingly impoverished countryside. The presence of permanent rather than migrant job-seekers represented a major demographic shift. So, too, did the growing numbers of economically independent women who evaded traditional patriarchal controls as well as government regulations by establishing themselves in informal occupations as washerwomen, shebeen keepers and prostitutes. Developments such as these significantly diminished the capacity of the state to exert control over Africans in the cities.

Vibrant forms of cultural expression flourished with the development of large, young and often unstable black urban communities. The growth of *marabi* music and township jazz, illegal beer brewing, gangsterism and independent Churches combined to increase Africans' sense of social autonomy; such developments also provided a receptive if volatile basis for the growth of new forms of identity and political awareness. Black workers in relatively secure industrial employment posed a different, but no less troubling, threat to the government as they joined the rapidly growing trades union movement and pressed for better living and employment conditions. By 1945 the Congress of Non-European Trade Unions represented over 150,000 workers in more than a hundred affiliated unions – even though the principle of African union membership was not officially recognised by the government.

For a brief period after 1942 the Smuts government responded to these social pressures by signalling that segregation was about to be reversed – a change of direction which appeared to be given substance by official relaxation of the pass laws and well-publicised moves to improve welfare and educational provision for Africans. The hopes and expectations that were aroused were sharpened by the war against fascism. Black soldiers and civilians saw themselves as participants in a war for international freedom and made direct connections between the fight for liberty in Europe and the liberation struggle at home.

Nationalist dreams were also inspired by a growing pan-Africanist consciousness which took note of Ethiopia's defiant defence of its sovereignty in the face of Italian aggression, as well as rising independence movements in Asia. This sentiment was very much in evidence at the landmark 1945 Manchester pan-African congress, which was attended by nationalist leaders from throughout the African continent.

The influence of international events on local thinking is immediately apparent in the ANC's seminal 1943 document *African Claims*. It was drafted by a committee that consciously sought to apply to South Africa the principles of the 1941 Atlantic Charter, in particular its stated commitment to sovereign rights and self-government for all oppressed peoples. *African Claims* thereby adopted a language and tone that contrasted markedly with the formal statements and petitions characteristic of previous ANC official discourse. What had hitherto been polite requests now became demands; appeals to restore the privileges enjoyed by 'civilised' Africans were rephrased in terms of a democratic 'bill of rights' applicable to all adult citizens; the citation of specific grievances requiring alleviation of injustices began to transmute into a broad social vision encompassing basic economic reforms, a 'fair' redistribution of land, and the provision of health and education services on an equal basis. This vision of the future presumed not only a more interventionist state, but also one in which the interests of the people as a whole were represented.

The social consequences of the war were especially evident in the industrialised Transvaal region which, more than ever before, dominated the political and economic pulse of the country. Among the most important expressions of social unrest at this time were countless localised instances of popular and community radicalism. The series of bus boycotts between 1940 and 1944 in the African township of Alexandra to the north of Johannesburg is a notable example. In an impressive display of community solidarity and determination many thousands of workers and domestic servants chose to walk up to twenty miles daily for weeks at a time rather than accept increased fares. Various liberal and left-wing political groupings, including the CPSA and the ANC, offered material assistance to the boycotters and sought to channel spontaneous popular anger into formal structures. However, the ANC as a whole remained generally aloof from events and did little to enhance its standing among ordinary workers. Indeed, a number of its most prominent leaders, including Xuma and R.G. Baloyi, regarded the crisis as an opportunity to enter the transport market themselves and were inclined to justify their entrepreneurial aspirations in the name of nationalism.

The emergence of squatters' movements in response to housing shortages and high rents constitutes another graphic example of resistance and assertion, although the ANC was again only peripherally involved in such activities. The most famous squatter leader was James Mpanza. Part visionary, part gangster, this raffish figure enjoined his community of followers, the *Sofasonke* ('We Shall Die'), to solve the housing crisis for themselves by defying municipal authority and occupying land in the environs of present-day Soweto. Squatters represented a serious threat to the authority of the state and its cherished hopes of orderly administration. But mutual mistrust between squatter leaders and political organisations like the ANC and CPSA made ongoing co-operation problematic. Squatters were suspicious of external control and tended to rely on leaders who were able to deliver real material assistance, rather than political figures whose stock-in-trade was abstract promises and theories.

Formal political organisations like the ANC operated with greater ease within the trade union movement which grew rapidly during the war years, but even here the ANC was an uncertain participant in events. An especially important development, given the centrality of the gold-mining industry to the South African economy, was the establishment of the African Mineworkers' Union in 1941 under the auspices of the Transvaal Congress and with strong support from the Communist Party. Individual ANC and Communist members like Edwin Mofutsanyana, Gaur Radebe, James Majoro and J.B. Marks played key roles in the creation and development of the Mineworkers' Union. The ANC took a firm stand in favour of a minimum wage and resolutely opposed discriminatory labour legislation. However, its leaders remained wary of identifying too closely with working-class militancy; they had evidently not yet abandoned their hope of gaining formal recognition as the representatives of organised African political opinion. Thus, in 1942, Xuma deplored strike action in view of the needs of the war effort and, in highly deferential language, offered to help the Smuts government to settle and prevent 'avoidable strikes'. Xuma's ambivalent support of working-class action was revealed again in 1946 when more than 70,000 African mineworkers struck in support of improved pay and working conditions. The strike was violently crushed by the police, and the trade union movement as a whole received a massive setback from which it only began to recover in the 1950s.

These examples highlight the difficulty of generalising about the ANC's responses to popular struggles during the 1940s. Congress was in the throes of transition into a radical mass nationalist movement, but it was neither organisationally nor ideologically unified. Moreover, the political orientation of its leadership was vigorously challenged by assertive young Africanist radicals, and by the Communist Party too. Congress remained regionally divided as well. Despite Xuma's best efforts to build up a central organisation, the provincial arms of Congress were largely independent and often wayward: regional representatives frequently operated beyond the control of the president-general and positioned themselves with respect to local political circumstances. Such problems were most acute in the Cape and Natal, where internal crises, leadership rivalries and ideological disputes threatened co-operation with Congress at a national level. Even in the Transvaal, where Congress's organisation was concentrated, the movement lacked coherence and, as several outstanding case studies have shown, its impact on local communities was varied. Any overall assessment of the ANC has therefore to take into consideration its involvement in specific instances of communal resistance. Nevertheless, it can safely be asserted that the ANC was increasingly engaging with popular struggles and adopting a more confrontational attitude towards the state. In contrast to the dormant and fractious decade of the 1930s, the 1940s pulsated with political energy.

The advent of the ANC Youth League in 1943–4 (including individuals such as Anton Lembede, Jordan Ngubane, Peter Mda, Nelson Mandela and Walter Sisulu) did much to reconfigure the ANC as a vigorous, modern mass movement. This process was accompanied by a protracted generational and ideological struggle which ultimately saw the Youth League prevail over Xuma's 'old guard'. Xuma himself had proved politically adept and retained considerable standing within the Youth League but, in 1949, when the conflict between the Youth League and the ANC establishment came to a head, he was replaced as president by Dr James Moroka, with Youth Leaguer Walter Sisulu acting as secretary-general. The Youth League's victory was an auspicious development with far-reaching consequences for the medium- and long-term prospects of the liberation movement. Indeed, in many respects the Youth League *was* the modern ANC. Its hold over the organisation proved tenacious even as its members aged: fifty years after its creation, Youth League veterans like Oliver Tambo, Walter Sisulu and Nelson Mandela (all of whom were Xhosa-speaking compatriots from the rural Eastern Cape) were among the core leadership who finally brought the ANC into government.

The guiding spirit and first president of the Youth League was Anton Lembede, a charismatic and intellectually gifted lawyer who arrived in Johannesburg in 1943 aged twenty-nine to serve articles in Pixley Seme's law firm. Born into an impoverished family of Natal sharecroppers, largely self-taught, and without advantageous social connections, Lembede's unusual rise to political prominence was paralleled by his unconventional social and philosophical attitudes. As the principal theorist of 'Africanism', Lembede advocated the need for black self-reliance and racial pride. With puritanical distaste, he disdained the cosmopolitan and sophisticated existence of black Johannesburg as evidence of moral degeneracy and cultural confusion, seeking the basis of black identity instead in an immanent 'African spirit' rooted in the soil and history of the continent. The mix of cultural and racial essentialism which suffuses Lembede's thought led him to proclaim Africa as 'a blackman's country'. He was inclined to reject political co-operation with white and Indian radicals and, notwithstanding a clear intellectual debt to various brands of European romantic nationalism, he denounced all foreign ideologies – communism in particular – as a threat to indigenous self-assertion.

Together with his close associate Peter Mda, Lembede exerted a profound influence on the Youth League. He provided it with a distinctive philosophical outlook which looked back to the Garveyism of the 1920s and laid the basis of a political legacy which the pan-Africanist and Black Consciousness movements of the 1950s and 1970s would later expand upon. Lembede's uncompromising brand of prophetic cultural nationalism was founded on a belief in the efficacy of spontaneous political arousal. His inspiring influence on the Youth League helped to orient the ANC as a whole towards mass action, but he had little interest in matters of political organisation or detailed strategy. This dimension of politics was far more evident in the case of Youth Leaguers like Sisulu, Mandela and Tambo, who were all varyingly influenced by Africanist ideals but increasingly demonstrated a pragmatic willingness to co-operate with Africanist as well as left-wing forces within the ANC. After Lembede's sudden death in 1947 it was this close grouping which overturned Xuma in 1949 and thereafter came to assume dominant positions in the ANC.

The responsibilities of leadership and the need to develop a common front against the Malan government after 1948 tended to moderate some of the more extreme examples of anti-white and anti-Indian sentiment emanating from within the Youth League. Beneath its energetic radicalism and militancy the League was by no means a tightly organised group sharing a single viewpoint. Willie Nkomo and Lionel Majombozi, for example, were Marxists. Others like Jordan Ngubane and Oliver Tambo were inclined towards a broader African nationalism which contrasted with the more exclusivist Africanism of Lembede and his associates. Nor did the League have full control over Congress. A sizeable left-wing constituency was represented by communists like J.B. Marks, Moses Kotane and Dan Tloome. The ANC's cautious tradition of liberal-inclined non-racialism was also very much in evidence in the shape of the influential Fort Hare academic Professor Z.K. Matthews as well as the continued presence of veteran leaders like James Moroka and Silas Molema.

The revival of the Communist Party in the 1940s mirrored the ascendancy of the Youth League but challenged it at the same time. The Soviet Union's entry into the war and Stalin's re-statement of the popular front against fascism considerably broadened the Communist Party's scope for political activity, widened its appeal, and afforded it a degree of respectability. During the war years Party membership rapidly increased, especially among Africans. Newspapers with communist sympathies were widely circulated. Industrial militancy and other forms of popular resistance provided the Party with important opportunities to establish its presence in trades unions and in specific campaigns such as the 1943–4 anti-pass law protests. Communists were represented most heavily in the Transvaal and in the Western Cape (though in the latter case the Stalinist CPSA was rivalled by the Trotskyite-aligned Unity Movement, to which many Coloured intellectuals gravitated). As the self-proclaimed vanguard of struggle against class and racial oppression, the Communist Party sought to influence and direct whichever 'progressive' forces it identified. With respect to the

ANC, the Party brought with it traditions of tactical acuteness, disciplined organisation and a firm commitment to non-racialism.

Relations were not always smooth. The Communist Party and Youth League were mutually suspicious and sometimes outright antipathetic. The 1947 'Doctors' Pact' struck between Dr Xuma of the ANC and Drs Naicker and Dadoo of the revived and newly radicalised Natal Indian Congress reflected a growing understanding of the need for all oppressed groups to unite in opposition to white supremacist rule – but it also served to exacerbate Youth League fears of growing non-African influence. Nevertheless, the differences between communists and Youth Leaguers were not always as clear-cut as might be assumed from official statements and political postures. Both were equally concerned to steer the ANC in a radical direction, and they were similarly supportive of militant action. The experience of working together against a common enemy often provided salutary reminders of whom one's friends really were. At a time of increasing opposition to white supremacist rule, tactical alliances and flexibility were willingly entered into. Independent-minded intellectuals like Joe Matthews, son of 'Z.K.', sought to incorporate Marxist theory into the framework of the Youth League's Africanism. And, after the death of Lembede, other Youth Leaguers such as Jordan Ngubane and Nelson

Mandela showed increasing willingness to absorb aspects of Marxist theory within a broad conception of African nationalism. Ideological divisions between communists and Africanists were real enough, but they were not impermeable, and individuals were apt to redefine their affiliations to particular camps according to circumstance.

In 1949 the Youth League unveiled its Programme of Action which was promptly adopted by the ANC as a whole. Building on the thinking of *African Claims* as well as its 1944 Manifesto, this document represented the culmination of the League's political work over the decade and served as a manifesto for campaigns of mass action in the 1950s. The Programme now defined the object of the ANC as the achievement of 'national freedom'; this was taken to mean 'freedom from white domination and the attainment of political independence', an ambiguous formulation that left a great deal open to debate. The new policy was not notably more radical than *African Claims* with respect to its social and economic demands, but it did commit the ANC to a campaign of boycotts, strikes and civil disobedience as well as a one-day national stoppage of work. To this extent, the Programme of Action marked a militant departure from previous ANC documents.

FOUR

Civil Disobedience and Defiance

The Programme of Action set the stage for the political campaigns of the 1950s. Whereas the radicalism of the 1920s had been followed by a long period of political quiescence, the 1950s consolidated and provided added political substance to the militant 1940s. The ANC was thereby confirmed as the dominant force of opposition to the apartheid state. In other respects, too, the 1950s represented a defining moment for the ANC. For the first time in its history the organisation was able to plan, lead and execute a systematic national campaign of political action. On the other hand, the failure of the campaign to realise the objective of defeating the government by peaceful means meant that this was the *last* time in its history that the ANC remained committed to achieving its objectives exclusively through methods of non-violence and civil action.

The pattern of politics for the 1950s was established in the opening two years of the decade. As we have seen, the Programme of Action set the ANC on a course of direct confrontation with the apartheid state. However, although the Malan government still commanded less than half the support of the white electorate and had not yet consolidated its own internal power base, the prospect of confrontation did not threaten it. On the contrary, the government viewed a wholesale assault on black political activity as one of the best ways of establishing its authority. In 1950 a slew of legislation was put through parliament. The Population Registration and Group Areas Acts together laid the foundations for the new apartheid system by allocating every individual at birth a defined racial category and providing the means to restrict racial groups to particular residential and business areas. The Suppression of Communism Act defined 'communism' in such an all-embracing manner that it could be, and was, construed to apply to virtually any radical form of opposition.

These draconian measures were immediately challenged by the ANC. On 1 May 1950 a national stay-away from work was called. It attracted considerable support, especially in the Transvaal, and led to violent clashes in which 18 Africans were killed and 30 injured. The May Day stay-away was notable as the first country-wide example of combined worker action. It was supported by the ANC president-general James Moroka as well as prominent activists such as J.B. Marks who maintained joint ANC and Communist affiliations. But Youth Leaguers like Mandela and Tambo denounced the event on the grounds that it was a communist-inspired effort to steal a march on the ANC's Programme of Action. Further discussions between nationalists and left-wingers within the ANC, as well as with members of the Indian Congress, culminated in a decision to hold a National Day of Protest and Mourning on 26 June 1950. The Youth League was fully behind the event and issued a fiery statement which declared that 'AFRICA'S CAUSE MUST TRIUMPH' and that 'VICTORY CANNOT BUT BE OURS.'

In contrast to the May Day experience, the response to the Day of Protest and Mourning in the Transvaal was poor, though local successes were claimed in particular townships. In the Xhosa-speaking Eastern Cape, where the ANC enjoyed long-established support, the stoppage was remarkably successful. Port Elizabeth was virtually brought to a halt and the stay-away was also highly effective in the Natal port city of Durban. A report to the ANC national executive frankly acknowledged that not all the desired results of the historic day had been achieved, but nevertheless claimed that 1950 had been 'a turning point in the political history of the African people in this country'.

This was fair comment. Although the strength of the apartheid state had in no way been seriously challenged, new forms of resistance were being tried out which would define the pattern of protest in the future. In the tactics of work stay-aways and boycotts that were emerging as staple forms of civil disobedience, Gandhian influences are readily detectable. (The Mahatma experimented with principles of *satyagraha* during his early years in South Africa and his presence continued to be felt via the Natal and later the South African Indian Congress.) Such forms of resistance had the advantage of avoiding head-on violent confrontation with the police. They allowed particular grievances to be expressed in terms of wider political principles, relied strongly on community initiative, and were flexible enough to be adapted to local circumstances.

At the leadership level, a notable development in planning and executing the Day of Protest and Mourning was the growing extent of co-operation between the ANC, the newly radicalised South African Indian Congress, the (Coloured) African Peoples Organisation, the Communist Party and the Council of Non-European Trade Unions. This convergence of political energies signified the emergence of what was soon to become known as the 'Congress Alliance': a multi-racial, ideologically heterodox and regionally representative confederation of extra-parliamentary opposition movements with the ANC at its centre, brought together by a common concern to liberate the mass of South Africans from increasing racial and class oppression.

The reaction of the apartheid government did much to promote the cohesiveness of this growing popular coalition whose broad anti-government sentiment was complemented by other mass campaigns such as those initiated by the Cape-based Franchise Action Council as well as two white-led ex-servicemen's organisations, the 'Torch Commando' and the Springbok Legion, formed by soldiers who discovered that they had won the war against fascism abroad only to find it reappearing at home. Concerned to demonstrate its power and to shore up its ethnic base by demonstrating no hint of weakness, the government gave the police unbridled authority to crack down on dissent with harsh measures involving large-scale arrests, tighter application of the pass laws, increased surveillance, and raids on opposition newspapers and organisations. Such actions had the dual effect of reducing the sphere of legitimate protest and criminalising large sections of the population. In addition, the government was now actively exploring mechanisms to remove the franchise rights of Coloured voters, an issue that hit particularly hard in the Cape. The way was therefore open for the ANC and its affiliate organisations to coalesce around opposition to 'unjust laws' and, in so doing, to build a broad alliance between different social and political groupings.

The government's indiscriminate anti-communism unwittingly played into the hands of the nascent liberation movement in other ways too. The Communist Party dissolved itself in 1950 in advance of official legislation. Its African members now integrated themselves more firmly into the ANC or, as was the case with white communists, established themselves in the Congress of Democrats (1953) which came to assume an influential position within the Congress Alliance on its own account. Divisions between Africanists and left-wingers within the ANC remained, but the practical necessity of working together had the effect of neutralising some of these antagonisms. Influential Youth Leaguers like Mandela and Sisulu began to work much more closely with non-African communists at this time. The effect of segregating white communists and left-wingers in the Congress of Democrats may also have helped to diminish African exclusivist fears of white infiltration into the ANC proper.

The Defiance Campaign of 1952 was a crucial moment in which the developing Congress Alliance came to test the potential and limits of mass civil disobedience. Plans emerged directly out of the experience of the June 1950 Day of Protest and involved a joint council carefully composed of two senior members of the African and Indian

Congresses apiece, with Moroka of the ANC acting as the chair. The Campaign was expressly directed against the rapidly expanding body of discriminatory legislation introduced by the Malan government. Of particular concern was the 1951 Bantu Authorities Act which laid the basis for the future *bantustans*, those self-governing 'tribal' states whose creation represented apartheid in its most hubristic form. In his final address as president of the ANC, in December 1951, Moroka outlined the terms and objectives of the Defiance Campaign. He called for 'democratic rights in this land of our birth' in a manner that evoked the familiar liberal Christian nationalism of the mainstream old ANC, while also paying careful attention to the different tendencies within the Congress Alliance. Thus, Moroka assured the government that 'we ask for nothing that is revolutionary', adding for good measure that if 'what we ask for is communistic, then communism is humane and Christian'. Moroka defined African nationalism in broadly inclusive terms and explicitly asserted Congress's preparedness to work with 'the Europeans, the Indians and the Coloureds' for the welfare of South Africa, as long as such co-operation was entered into on the basis of equal partnership.

Official letters from Moroka and Sisulu to Malan carefully explaining the objectives of the Defiance Campaign were arrogantly cast aside: as far as the government was concerned, the ANC did not have the right to approach the prime minister directly, but should rather address any grievances it had via the Department of Native Affairs. Not only was the state rejecting Congress's specific demands, it was rejecting the very notion that Congress represented anything more than the views of agitators and communists. Evidently, the state could not even contemplate the idea that Congress and its affiliates had a part in the country's future. In order to remind whites of the political aspirations and nationalist claims of black South Africans, the opening phase of the Defiance Campaign was timed to coincide with the climax of the officially sponsored 1952 Van Riebeeck celebrations. Thus, just as whites celebrated the tercentenary of colonial settlement in an orgy of pageant and self-congratulation, the leaders of the Defiance Campaign called on their followers to mark 6 April as a National Day of Pledge and Prayer. A more dramatic expression of two competing nationalisms could hardly have been arranged.

The official starting date of the Defiance Campaign was 26 June, the anniversary of the 1950 Day of Protest. Volunteers were enjoined to pledge to serve their country and their people in the Campaign for the Defiance of Unjust Laws. Groups of volunteers displaying the thumbs-up salute and shouting 'Afrika' and 'Mayibuye' were deputed to

41

defy the pass laws and ignore apartheid regulations at park benches, railway stations, post offices and other segregated institutions. The hope was that by inviting arrest and imposing intolerable burdens on the capacity of the state to police apartheid regulations, the system would be rendered inoperable. Mass rallies and marches were also planned, along with church services, prayer meetings and other public expressions of moral strength.

The first planned acts of defiance took place in Johannesburg and Port Elizabeth on 26 June and soon spread to other towns and cities throughout the country. Between June and December over 8,000 resisters were arrested and jailed. By far the largest number of arrests took place in the Eastern Cape. The Transvaal also figured prominently, though there were fewer than 200 arrests recorded in each of the provinces of Natal and the Orange Free State. The preponderance of defiance activities in the Eastern Cape is striking – all the more so because rural areas as well as urban centres were involved. There is no simple way of explaining the Eastern Cape's prominence in the Defiance Campaign, though it is undoubtedly of significance that political awareness was already highly developed in this region, so deeply marked as it was by early colonial conquest, established educational institutions, and widespread rural poverty. In view of the heavily Johannesburg-centric orientation of the

ANC, the political dynamism of the Eastern Cape stood out as a reminder that the national leadership should not lose sight of Congress's historic grassroots support base. Inevitably, this disparity was a source of ongoing provincial and ethnic tensions.

Whether the originators of the Defiance Campaign intended the protests as a way of sharpening political awareness and increasing mass mobilisation or whether they hoped that it might prompt the imminent collapse of the apartheid system is difficult to determine. There is evidence for both interpretations, but the former is by far the most likely. For many participants, passive resistance was a political tactic that fitted in closely with traditions of Christian sacrifice and moral assertion; for others, it was a necessary stage in a process that would prepare the way for genuine revolutionary struggle. However, political conditions were not yet conducive to sustaining such an insurrection, and the capacity of the state to contain incidents of urban violence was not seriously tested. Notably, the Campaign began to falter towards the end of 1952 when riots broke out in Port Elizabeth and elsewhere. The violence was immediately condemned by the ANC and proved personally troubling to its new president, Albert Luthuli, who succeeded the conservative and politically discredited James Moroka at this time.

The Defiance Campaign was conducted with remarkable restraint and discipline. One index of its success is that membership of the ANC grew rapidly during 1952 (a figure of 100,000 is often mentioned, though precise figures are impossible to come by). As a result, Congress was able to confirm its claim to be the pre-eminent element in the anti-apartheid movement and to reaffirm its commitment to strategies of mass mobilisation. An important precedent for future co-operation with sympathetic Indians, Coloureds and Whites had also been established. Within the country the rituals of struggle and the heady experience of direct confrontation with the authorities constituted a powerful political and symbolic legacy which remained in the popular imagination for long after. Externally, the establishment of a United Nations commission on the South African racial situation indicated the beginnings of serious international concern about the human injustices of apartheid. These were all important gains for the liberation movement and proved vitally important in sustaining the ANC in its long years of exile after 1960.

Notwithstanding its successes, the experience of the Defiance Campaign highlighted serious organisational deficiencies and examples of political inexperience. In particular, the relative quiescence of key areas in the country could not be ignored. Nor could it be claimed that the security of the apartheid state had been seriously threatened. Tellingly, not one of the 'unjust laws' was repealed. Instead, parliament hurriedly passed new measures to contain protest. One of these sanctioned whipping as punishment for political dissent. Another provided for the imposition of a state of emergency to maintain public order. The government also reacted with a flurry of banning orders, arrests and trials that shattered the alliance leadership and led to the demise of Moroka's presidency. Just as the liberation movement had learned from the experience of mass action, so the state was engaged in refining its repertoire of repression. By the end of 1952 the momentum of the campaign had largely been halted. And in the election of 1953 the government greatly strengthened its electoral position.

FIVE

The Congress of the People and the Freedom Charter

With only a brief pause after 1952, the political upheaval of the 'long' 1950s continued unabated until the climactic tragedy of Sharpeville in 1960. During this crowning era of mass politics the ANC enjoyed a higher profile than it had ever achieved or was to achieve again until the 1980s. Like Harlem of the 1920s, black Johannesburg exuded a confident and glamorous cosmopolitanism. Its compelling township jazz rhythms, its breezy literary and journalistic culture, even its stylish (though undoubtedly predatory) gangsterism stand out as the cultural counterparts of political defiance. At the heart of this political and cultural effervescence was the black freehold area of Sophiatown, home to many of the leading social, cultural and political figures of the day. The battle to save Sophiatown and the Western Areas townships from the encroaching white suburbs and the bulldozers of the state was lost by 1955. Few seriously imagined the outcome could have been otherwise. The government revelled in its power by building a white working-class suburb on the ruins of Sophiatown and naming it Triomf – 'Triumph'. But despite ending in defeat, the struggle for Sophiatown encapsulates the powerful spirit of community resistance which was so conspicuous a feature of the time. So, too, do the bus boycotts at Evaton and Alexandra which revived the transport radicalism of the previous decade. One of the most evocative images of the 1950s was the epic march of thousands of women who converged on the government in Pretoria in 1956 to demand an end to the pass laws in a daring and defiant statement of female anger and outrage.

These highly visible (though sometimes overly romanticised) spectacles of cultural and political resistance to the entrenchment of apartheid bulk large in the political memory of the 1950s. They should not, however, obscure what has been referred to as the 'hidden' struggles of rural black South Africans. In their concern to deny the apartheid government's insistence that 'natives' were naturally 'tribal' and should be confined to the rural bantustans, the urban black intelligentsia of the 1940s and 1950s was apt to treat rural Africans with a measure of condescension or disdain – an attitude curiously paralleled by revolutionary theorists and academic writers whose primary focus has been on proletarian class-formation and industrial conflict. A distinct urban bias was undoubtedly evident in the orientation of the ANC and the Communist Party as well.

Govan Mbeki was one ANC leader who constantly argued the case for greater political involvement in the rural areas. Like other perceptive observers, Mbeki understood that there was no hermetic seal between town and countryside – as the success of the Defiance Campaign in the eastern Cape demonstrated. Ongoing political and cultural exchange between town and country was maintained through a complex process of osmosis, in which the migrant labour system, youth associations and kinship networks were important agencies. Among the more dramatic manifestations of rural rebellion and militancy in the 1950s were the armed refusal of Witzieshoek peasants to comply with cattle-culling in 1950, the outright refusal of Bafarutshe women to carry passes in 1957, the Sekhukuneland uprising of 1958–9, and the protracted 1960 Pondoland revolt against the imposition of apartheid rural government structures which Govan Mbeki eloquently detailed in *South Africa: The Peasants' Revolt* (Harmondsworth, 1964, p. 130). In his view the Pondo movement 'succeeded by example in accomplishing what discussion had failed to do in a generation – convincing the leadership of the importance of the peasants in the reserves to the entire national struggle'

Notwithstanding this upsurge of resistance, the political initiative remained with the apartheid government, whose power and control over black South Africans continued to be extended and enforced ever more systematically. The ANC, though highly visible and capable of mounting significant acts of protest, was in defensive mode after 1952. Its rapid growth in membership and support put further strain on an already severely stretched administrative machine which was often chaotic, lacking in secure funding, and inappropriately geared towards survival in a climate of increasing repression. As leader of the ANC for most of the 1950s, Albert Luthuli, a teacher, lay Methodist preacher and elected Christian chief from rural Zululand, showed great personal and moral courage: he was a dignified and inspiring exponent of the politics of passive resistance and was the first South African to be awarded the Nobel Peace Prize. But for several reasons, including ill-health and official restrictions on his movements, Luthuli's day-to-day grip on ANC affairs was often tenuous and his liberal Christian pacifism could not easily be reconciled with the move to more militant forms of confrontation later in the decade.

One notable attempt to rectify the organisational deficiences of the ANC and to adjust to the increasingly harsh political climate of oppression was Mandela's 'M-plan', a semi-clandestine scheme to create tightly knit street 'cells' with clear lines of authority and strong discipline. The plan was never fully operationalised. Its fame seems to derive partly from its author, as well as the fact that in subsequent years it became mutually advantageous for ANC combatants and the state to depict Congress as an underground revolutionary organisation. The ANC's limitations were particularly exposed in its response to the 1953 Bantu Education Act. This notorious measure was designed to eradicate the influence of independent church and mission schools and to provide Africans with a cheap form of mass education and training geared towards the production of a subservient labour force. It represented an unprecedented assault on Africans' aspirations and a direct attack on teachers, who constituted one of the mainstays of the African middle class. But although the ANC denounced the provisions of the hated Bantu education legislation, supported school boycotts and attempted to organise 'cultural clubs' offering alternative schooling, it was unable either to produce a credible counter-strategy to the government or to match its own grandiloquent rhetoric with coherent action.

Along with the Defiance Campaign, the ANC's most imaginative initiative was undoubtedly the Congress of the People, held in the open veld outside

Johannesburg in 1955. This event marked the public consummation of Alliance or 'Charterist' politics. Nearly 3,000 delegates of all colours and backgrounds attended the proceedings in a carnival-like show of popular strength, despite considerable police harrassment and severe logistical encumbrances. The Congress culminated in the adoption of a powerful ten-point Freedom Charter which affirmed a host of liberal-democratic freedoms. Among these were the right of the people to govern, to share in the country's wealth, to enjoy human rights and equality before the law, and to enjoy equal access to education, housing and medical care.

These aspirations were relatively uncontroversial. Rather more problematic were two studiedly ambiguous provisions: the statement that 'South Africa belongs to all who live in it, black and white', and the provisions to transfer into common ownership the country's mineral wealth, banks and monopoly industries. The Africanist element within the ANC resented the implication that Africans did not have prior and superior rights to the country (though this was often dressed up in a confusing discourse about the difference between multi-racialism and non-racism); on the question of economic nationalisation, liberals, Marxists and Africanists engaged in extended polemics as to whether the wealth clause amounted to a pseudo-communist manifesto. These were not merely abstract debates. Their revolutionary implications were exhaustively tested in court during the 1956–61 treason trial, and served as the basis of fundamental and passionate debate within the general anti-apartheid movement through the 1950s and again in the 1980s. Debate was further fuelled by disputes surrounding the drafting of the Freedom Charter. Its champions insisted that it was drawn up in an open and democratic manner and that it directly reflected the popular will. On the other hand, anti-communists maintained that its formulation was controlled and manipulated by a small group of white Marxists under the guiding hand of Lionel 'Rusty' Bernstein.

The principal sponsors of the 1955 Congress were the ANC, the Indian Congress, the Coloured People's Organisation and the Congress of Democrats. This alliance came to be expressed iconographically by a wheel with four spokes, an image whose choice may have been influenced by the Congress Party in India. The four organisations which comprised the alliance were broadly representative of the four principal racial groups of the country. This conscious construction of multi-racialism mirrored the official racial categories of the state – a sharp irony that advocates of non-racialism were quick to seize upon. Two other organisations soon became integral partners in the alliance: the Federation of South African Women, established in 1954, and the South African Congress of Trade Unions (SACTU), formed in 1955.

SACTU emerged out of a complex history of racially divided unions and a highly discriminatory legal framework in which Africans were not even recognised as 'employees'. The notion that workers' economic struggles were intimately related to their broader political rights and ambitions was accepted as an axiom. But what did it mean to be a political trade union movement? At its inauguration, SACTU represented more than 35,000 workers in some thirty unions grouped within the manufacturing, service and transport sectors. However, the bulk of its membership was narrowly concentrated in a handful of large, established unions which jealously guarded their autonomy. The political demands made of workers by the nationalist movement were often at odds with the views of orthodox trade unionists, who saw their prime imperative as building and maintaining strong and effective workplace organisation. On the other hand, left-wing critics argued that SACTU was merely an adjunct of the nationalist or bourgeois-oriented ANC, and argued that the proper role of trade unions was to provide a platform for working-class leadership of the anti-apartheid movement.

These disputes were greatly intensified by the Communist Party's development of the theory of 'internal colonialism' during the early 1950s (in the wake of the party's disbandment and secret reconstitution). The late 1920s' doctrine of the 'independent native republic' was now reformulated in terms of a new thesis which argued in pragmatic but opaque fashion that South Africa's configuration of race and class evinced a unique 'colonialism of a special type'. This entailed that, as a necessary condition for the emergence of true socialism, class struggle had to be sublimated to the needs of national struggle. Abstruse as some of the finer points of the arguments were, they had a fundamental bearing on the conception of left-wingers' relationship to the Congress alliance and of the primacy of working-class struggle within it. Also at issue in this debate (though mostly unstated) was the place of non-African activists within the liberation movement.

The relationship between the Federation of South African Women (FSAW) and the ANC Alliance was beset by analogous tensions and dilemmas. Like SACTU, the FSAW was an umbrella body representing women in the ANC Women's League, trade unions and community organisations. The FSAW concentrated its energies on opposing the extension of pass laws to women and resisting the imposition of Bantu education and the Group Areas Act. It was involved in many campaigns, sometimes on its own account, but often in association with other protest movements. In its role as a campaigning organisation the FSAW proved highly successful, partly as a result of the inspirational leadership of individuals like Lilian Ngoyi, Helen Joseph and Ray Alexander, but also through the adoption of imaginative tactics which deliberately exploited the supposed weakness and innocence of women in order to challenge or mock the power of men. During the great 1956 march to Pretoria, as many as 20,000 women converged at the Union Buildings chanting a fearsome warning to the prime minister: 'Strydom, you have tampered with the women, you have struck a rock. You will be crushed!'

The politics of gender were in some respects deeply conservative. For instance, many men resented passes for women as an encroachment by the state upon traditional patriarchal rights, while women often couched opposition to government action in terms of a defence of their roles as wives and mothers. This did not mean that women accepted that they should be merely passive. On the contrary, politically active women inverted stereotypes of female weakness by shaming pass-carrying African men for their loss of masculinity. 'Give us your pants, the women will wear them!' was a popular and provocative taunt. But although the strength of women was affirmed by such language and gestures, the nature of women's subordination in what has been referred to as a 'patchwork' of patriarchal relationships was not seriously questioned; if anything, it was in their roles as conservative defenders of the family unit that protesting women were most effective and united. The FSAW's principal loyalty was to the wider Congress agenda, and calls for women's rights were invariably secondary to the requirements of the national liberation movement. Feminist concerns about patriarchal attitudes, birth control or women's roles within the domestic sphere could not easily be addressed within this context. Thus, although the federal nature of alliance politics conceded a separate political and social domain to women, the FSAW operated under a form of licence which ensured that it was incorporated within the Congress Alliance only as a junior partner.

The state's response to the Freedom Charter was a massive crackdown on extra-parliamentary organisations, and the arraignment on trial for treason of 156 leading activists drawn from a variety of different organisations and political constituencies. The methods of the special branch police in this show trial were indicative of the state's increasing intolerance towards any form of political dissent. In the view of the prosecutors, the aim of the Charterists was nothing less than the violent overthrow of the state. Sufficient legal protections nevertheless remained for the liberation movement to use this show trial to its own advantage. Massive public support and publicity were given to the defendants, who skilfully used courtroom procedure to publicise the anti-apartheid message. After a long drawn-out trial which finally ended in 1961, the defendants were acquitted.

Although the Treason Trial provided good publicity for the liberation movement and provided an opportunity for leaders of the Congress alliance to confer with each other, it absorbed political energies, disrupted the momentum of popular mobilisation and created a serious power vacuum within the ANC. Dissent, rivalries and disquiet about financial irregularities and an absence of internal democracy began to surface openly. These were not easily rebutted. Especially serious was the renewed pressure exerted by Africanist-inclined Youth Leaguers who were highly critical of the political turn taken by the ANC Alliance and were now poised to reassert the radical nationalist agenda of Lembede and Mda.

The Africanists charged that the nationalist tenets set out in the Programme of Action had been subverted by the multi-racialism of the Freedom Charter. In their view, the primary conflict in South Africa ought to be defined racially, between Africans and whites, conquered and conquerors. They regarded the proposition that the oppressed were fighting against an 'unjust system' as a Marxist abstraction which permitted non-Africans to pose as the 'friends of the natives' (much as earlier generations of liberals had done). The overall effect was to blunt the edge of the fight against white domination. Africans, it was argued, should rely on their own resources, develop their own pride, and lead their own struggle. They should disdain assistance from non-Africans and avoid the corrosive charms of social interaction with indulgent white sympathisers. Africans should instead cultivate a distinctive consciousness and seek inspiration in their indigenous culture and their heroes. In refining this message, Africanists steered a delicate line between racial chauvinism and the somewhat improbable claim that theirs was the only true form of non-racism. They sought to connect directly with what they took to be the gut instincts of ordinary Africans, in the conviction that once a true Africanist consciousness was aroused a spontaneous wave of popular insurgency would sweep whites from power.

SIX

Towards Sharpeville

The Africanist tendency was concentrated in Johannesburg, and this is where its challenge to the ANC was initially expressed. Dissent became manifest in 1954 when one of the Africanist leaders, Potlako Leballo, was expelled from the Orlando branch of the Youth League after insisting that the ANC return to its nationalist fundamentals. During the course of a fractious meeting of the Transvaal Congress in 1958 (which very nearly took a violent turn), long-standing tensions came to a head and a group of Africanists, excluded from the proceedings, broke with the ANC and its multi-racial Alliance. Secession soon followed in other ANC branches. In April 1959 the Pan-African Congress (PAC) was formally constituted under the leadership of Robert Sobukwe who, though not yet thirty-five, was already a highly respected leader. Sobukwe had been born to a poor but educationally ambitious family in the Karroo town of Graaff-Reinet and went on to attend Healdtown School and the University of Fort Hare before taking a post as a teacher of Zulu at the University of the Witwatersrand. His reflective style and intellectual gravitas complemented well the combative emotionalism of Leballo and Josias Madzunya.

In leaving the ANC, the pan-Africanists might easily have gone the way of other dissident break-away groups into swift oblivion. Loyalty to the organisation and respect for institutional continuity was much prized by the ANC. But the PAC was not just any splinter group. In Sobukwe, Leballo, Mda, Raboroko and Madzunya it possessed a strong and vigorous, albeit exclusively male, leadership. The PAC was well positioned to capitalise on the evident weaknesses of the ANC, including recent failures such as the desultory popular response to the 1958 stay-away call. It was also careful to stress that it was the natural inheritor of the true ANC message as enshrined in the Programme of Action – adopting the ANC's green, black and gold colours for good measure. The PAC's political message was powerful and direct. Its anti-communism, while principally a coded criticism of the undue influence of the Congress of Democrats and the Communist Party on the ANC, was ideally positioned to generate international support as the Cold War intensified. Even more important, its pan-Africanist message was in tune with the surge for independence in other parts of Africa. This was made clear at the

60

PAC's inaugural meeting when Kwame Nkrumah and Sékou Touré sent their greetings. If leaders like these had been able to deliver their countries to freedom, might the pan-Africanist message not do the same for South Africa?

The PAC set itself targets of a membership of 100,000 within a year, and liberation for South Africa by 1963. Neither objective was met, though the number of adherents it could claim by 1960, over 20,000, was comparable to the likely membership of the ANC at this time. The two organisations were now set on a competitive course to prove their political credentials, with the PAC keen to seize the initiative. In December 1959 both the PAC and the ANC separately announced plans for the start of an anti-pass campaign. Their objectives were very similar but, unlike the principled moral pacifism expressed by Luthuli, the PAC's insistence on non-violence was largely determined by tactical considerations. Its campaigning slogan, 'No bail, no defence, no fine', signalled a style of politics that was altogether more confrontational and uncompromising than that of the ANC. The PAC alleged that the ANC had frequently acted to constrain mass opposition; by contrast, its own brand of forthright radical nationalism and the unwavering example of its leaders would help to unleash deep-seated popular passions and thereby help ordinary people to free themselves.

The PAC announced 21 March 1960 as the start of its anti-pass campaign, deliberately pre-empting the ANC's demonstrations by a week. The PAC's support base and organisation was uncertain and untried, but it had succeeded in establishing a bridgehead in the industrial region of Vereeniging, south of Johannesburg. It was here that thousands of protesters converged on the police station of Sharpeville. Low-flying jets did not intimidate the crowd as they did elsewhere. Police panicked and opened fire without authority on the unarmed protesters, killing 69 and wounding more than 180. Most victims were shot in the back.

The Sharpeville massacre spurred further unrest and intensified the anti-pass campaign in other parts of the country. In Cape Town, where the PAC had also succeeded in establishing support, thousands of anti-pass protesters also gathered on 21 March, and although they initially dispersed when confronted by police, there was rioting later in the day. ANC president Luthuli declared 28 March a day of mourning to be observed by a national stay-away. International condemnation was swift. In an unprecedented move, the United Nations blamed the South African government for the killings. The government, unsettled as never before, moved to outlaw the ANC and PAC, declared a state of emergency and arrested hundreds of leaders, including Sobukwe and Leballo. It also announced a temporary suspension of the pass laws. This was the first time in modern South African history that political protests had yielded such tangible results. Most of the credit for this achievement accrued to the PAC rather than the ANC.

The tide of popular insurgency culminated in Cape Town on 30 March, when 30,000 marchers converged on the police headquarters in Cape Town, led by a young student and PAC activist, Philip Kgosana. Faced with a highly volatile situation and guided by Patrick Duncan, a prominent member of the Liberal Party, Kgosana decided to defuse the tension by persuading the crowd to disperse on the promise of a meeting with the Justice Minister. However, when he arrived for his appointment that evening, Kgosana was arrested. The strikes in the Cape Town area continued; however, the police surrounded the townships in a military cordon and crushed further resistance. Processions and pass-burnings by Africans in Durban and Port Elizabeth were also contained, but not without further deaths. The pass laws were reinstated and on 8 April the ANC and PAC were both banned.

In three weeks of unprecedented mass protests, of which the Sharpeville massacre and Cape Town marches were the cataclysmic centrepieces, the country's future was placed in the balance. This was no more a revolutionary moment than the white

worker's strike of 1922 had been. But it did
represent a crisis of unprecedented proportions: the
government was shaken, the police temporarily lost
control of Cape Town, a state of emergency had
been declared, and concessions had briefly been
forced on the pass laws. The serious political
situation was further exacerbated by large-scale
capital flight and prognostications of imminent
revolutionary upheaval. Yet, in demonstrating the
vulnerability of white supremacist rule, Sharpeville
also revealed weaknesses in the ANC and PAC. Most
important, the strategic limitations of non-violent
resistance were exposed. With the liberation
movements driven underground, the ANC's need
for a military capability became inescapable. It was
also apparent that the struggle would henceforth
have to take on an international dimension. It was to
advance this aim that Oliver Tambo secretly left the
country to establish an external mission of the ANC.

It took until 1964 for the post-Sharpeville political
situation to clarify. Resistance was not immediately
quelled and in some areas it intensified. In the
Transkci a remarkable phase of armed resistance to
the imposition of apartheid tribal structures,
increased taxation and enforced conservation
measures, known as the Pondoland revolt,
continued through most of 1960. There were other
sporadic outbreaks of rural rebellion and violence in
the Transkci and Ciskei from 1960 to 1963. The

Communist Party now announced its reformation as an underground organisation and publicly reaffirmed its commitment to the two-stage revolution. For its part, the ANC began to activate the cellular 'M-plan', albeit without much success. There were faltering moves, but attempts none the less, to create a broad anti-apartheid movement encompassing the ANC, PAC and Liberals. In May 1961 a last-gasp campaign of civil disobedience was organised by the so-called National Action Council, under the leadership of Mandela, to protest against Verwoerd's decision to transform South Africa into a republic. The planned stay-away met with only limited success and was called off on the second day.

SEVEN

The Struggle Moves Underground

Both banned liberation movements moved quickly to establish their own guerrilla organisations. During the course of 1961 the ANC formed a separate armed wing, Umkhonto we Sizwe ('The Spear of the Nation'), under Mandela's leadership. Umkhonto (MK) began operations in December and launched over 200 small-scale attacks throughout the country over the next eighteen months. Its largely symbolic sabotage campaign was restricted to blowing up strategic installations like pylons, railway lines and government offices. By contrast, the PAC's armed wing, Poqo ('Standing Alone' or 'Pure'), adopted a far more direct and bloody strategy during its campaign of 1962–3. Poqo did not shy away from killing people and hoped, through its attacks and assassinations in the Cape, to arouse a general state of revolutionary insurrection (akin to the theory of violence prescribed by the Algerian revolutionary Frantz Fanon). A third sabotage campaign was embarked upon by the African Resistance Movement. The efforts of this small and predominantly white group, composed of Liberal Party radicals and Trotskyites, were brought to an abrupt end as a result of an explosion in 1964 which killed a commuter at Johannesburg station and severely wounded several others.

The effectiveness of these experimental acts of violence was limited. Poqo's killing of whites aroused far more fear than the scantly reported accounts of isolated Umkhonto explosions. The move to sabotage was as much an expression of desperation and a declaration of future intent as a considered intensification of the anti-apartheid struggle. And in the case of the ANC, whose leader Albert Luthuli famously asserted that 'The road to freedom is via the Cross', it proved a difficult decision to take. Indecision was not, however, a feature of the Verwoerd government, which rapidly assumed the political initiative after the immediate shock of Sharpeville. Investor confidence rapidly returned, and by 1961 the country was embarked on a sustained economic boom which continued for over a decade. Verwoerd's swaggering decision to leave the Commonwealth and to establish a republic fulfilled a long-standing Afrikaner dream. It was also interpreted as a fitting riposte to Macmillan's lofty warning that a 'wind of change' was blowing over Africa. The government felt confident enough to lift the state of emergency (outside of Pondoland) after 1960. It enormously increased the powers of the security police and used new enabling legislation such as the 1962 Sabotage Act and the 1963 'Ninety Days' Act (which provided for long periods of solidary detention) to devastating effect. Ordinary Africans felt the burden of defeat rather more than their leaders, who were caught up in the excitement of clandestine activities. Those protestors who had burned their passes faced the humiliation of queuing up for replacement documents.

The acquittal of the Treason Trial defendants in 1961 proved a pyrrhic victory for the ANC. Two years later, in a spectacular police raid at a farm at Rivonia in northern Johannesburg, most of the Umkhonto 'high command' was arrested, along with extensive documentation relating to its plans for guerrilla action. Further arrests followed. The amateurism of the Rivonia revolutionaries contrasted with the clinical counter-insurgency strategy of the government and illustrated how unprepared the ANC was for its new role as an underground organisation. Until his arrest in 1962, Mandela had been conducting a spectacular one-man game of subterfuge during which he travelled abroad, met international statesmen, and undertook a short course of military training in Algeria. His adoption of disguises and habit of making surprise public appearances led to his becoming known as the 'Black Pimpernel'. There was a strong element of bravado about Mandela's actions, but his political authority was undoubtedly in the ascendant.

At the Rivonia trial of 1964 the defendants (who included Mandela, Sisulu, Mhalaba, Govan Mbeki, Kathrada, Bernstein and Motsoaledi) were charged with high treason. Their defence was conducted by Bram Fischer, an Afrikaner communist whose grandfather had been president of the Orange Free State. Mandela's commanding physical presence, personal dignity and leadership qualities came to the fore during the trial. Most impressive of all was his statement from the dock, a *cri de coeur* that was immediately recognised as a historic declaration of his own and the ANC's conception of the liberation struggle. Here Mandela reviewed his personal political career, explained the ANC's reluctant resort to violence, and reviewed the reasons behind the decision to form MK. He paid particular attention to the relationship between the ANC and the Communist Party, denying the state's contention that the aims of the two organisations were identical, while affirming their close co-operation in the common fight against oppression. Mandela defined himself as an African nationalist, as a 'patriot', and as an opponent of all forms of racism. He ended with a ringing peroration:

> During my lifetime I have dedicated myself to this
> struggle of the African people. I have fought against
> White domination, and I have fought against black
> domination. I have cherished the ideal of a democratic
> and free society in which all persons live together in
> harmony and with equal opportunities. It is an ideal
> which I hope to live for and to achieve. But if needs be, it
> is an ideal for which I am prepared to die. (T. Karis *et al.*,
> *From Protest to Challenge: A Documentary History of African
> Politics in South Africa 1882–1964*, vol. 3, Stanford, 1977,
> p. 796)

For at least a decade after 1964 the ANC virtually
ceased to exist in South Africa and the prospects for
liberation appeared more remote than ever. Writing
in 1974, those judicious and knowledgeable
academic chroniclers of the anti-apartheid struggle,
Thomas Karis and Gail Gerhart, struck a highly
pessimistic note: Mandela, Sisulu and Mbeki, they
reported, were languishing in the bleak surroundings
of Robben Island, serving out life sentences;
Sobukwe, though released from the Island, was
under close surveillance in Kimberley; Tambo,
the acting president of the ANC, was in exile;
Leballo was desperately trying to hold together the
remnants of the PAC from his base in Dar es
Salaam.

Inside the Republic, the pall of police surveillance and the prevalence of informers inhibit discussion of past political movements that have been described for more than a decade in white South African parlance as "terrorist". More and more, the leaders of the earlier years become shadowy figures. (*From Protest to Challenge*, vol. 3, pp. 684–5)

This sense of despair was shared by all but the most optimistic observers. Under the leadership of Hendrik Verwoerd white minority rule seemed more secure and arrogant than ever. During the 1960s South Africa's annual 6 per cent economic growth rate was exceeded only by Japan, and white South Africans had become among the most affluent groups in the world. The era of 'grand apartheid' saw the inauguration of massive schemes of social engineering. From 1960 the government pressed relentlessly ahead with its plan to divide the African population into ten 'ethnic' groups and to allocate each of these a self-governing rural bantustan. (The first, Transkei, was given 'independence' in 1976.) In pursuit of the bantustan strategy and in order to enforce the principle that blacks had no rights to be in 'white' cities other than as labourers, an elaborate programme of population removals was inaugurated. By 1983 perhaps 3.5 million Africans (as well as Coloureds and Indians) were compulsorily removed in pursuit of urban or rural resettlement plans. An extensive network of labour bureaux sprang up throughout the country to regulate and control the flow of African labour to towns, cities and farms. Although scholars are now agreed that apartheid was not implemented according to a grand Verwoerdian plan and that the system was continually wracked with internal contradictions and inconsistencies, widespread contemporary perceptions of a monolithic and indomitable state were not altogether misplaced.

What was the ANC doing during this period? For the most part it was attempting to secure its position as the leading anti-apartheid organisation and to survive into the future, although the organisation's capacity to do so was anything but assured. There were several dimensions to the ANC's existence at this time. London became the centre of its external mission, and widespread diplomatic connections were cultivated by Tambo. Forward bases were established in African 'front-line' states. The ANC forged a close association with the British Anti-Apartheid Movement, formed in 1959–60, which worked ceaselessly to mobilise liberal opinion, the Churches and sympathetic politicians against the apartheid regime. Oliver Tambo proved adept at international diplomacy and sought to position the ANC to take advantage of Cold War rivalries. However, this was a difficult balancing act to maintain, especially during the first two decades of exile. The ANC's intimate relationship with the Communist Party meant that it could rely on substantial ideological, military and financial help from the Soviet Union. But this came at a cost, for antagonists were easily able to dismiss the ANC as a communist satellite. Later, the situation became more fluid as Cold War politics became more complex and as international opinion hardened against the South African government. In the post-1976 period the ANC began more assiduously to cultivate links with liberal and anti-imperial sentiment in Britain and Scandinavia as well as at the United Nations. Oliver Tambo's pragmatism, collective leadership style and deep Christian beliefs were a source of particular strength at this time, allowing the ANC to function as a broad coalition and to lay claim to the moral high ground.

For the ANC leadership incarcerated on Robben Island, the period after Rivonia was particularly hard. In his remarkable autobiography, *Long Walk to Freedom* (London, 1994), Mandela called these the 'dark years'. On top of the severe privations of prison life, the daily racist indignities (which extended to the provision of food and clothing), the conditions of hard labour and the sense of personal and political isolation, there was a constant struggle to maintain morale and political purpose. A steady stream of new prisoners as well as the occasional smuggled newspaper, letter or visit helped the Islanders to keep abreast of political developments. For the most part, however, they were thrown back on their own resources, gradually developing organisational structures and discussion groups which led them to refer to Robben Island as a 'University'. Rivalries and tensions between prisoners with different political affiliations were often intense, especially where the PAC and ANC were concerned. Political debates among the ANC cadres could be acrimonious: the implications of the Sino–Soviet split, the nature of the relationship between Congress and the Communist Party and the question of working-class leadership of the struggle proved particularly contentious. Political differences were often exacerbated by personality conflicts. Although the new arrivals did not always accept the political authority of the Rivonia generation, a political hierarchy did coalesce around figures like Mandela, Sisulu, Mbeki, Mhlaba, Maharaj and Kathrada. As was the case in other nationalist struggles in Africa, imprisonment was a formative political experience: it created lasting bonds of trust, invested an absent leadership with moral legitimacy and mystique, and saved leaders from making the inescapable mistakes and compromises that ordinary engagement with politics involves.

A third sphere of ANC activity was the armed struggle led by the MK. Flat terrain, well-defended borders, a declining independent peasantry, and a vigilant white farming population did not favour the sort of guerrilla war that was so important a feature of liberation struggles in Mozambique or Zimbabwe. The military bases established in Tanzania were inadequately supplied, ill-disciplined and poorly motivated. Worst of all, cadres had little to do. One response to this malaise was a military alliance struck between MK and the Zimbabwean African People's Union. Joint operations against the white Rhodesian regime began on a small scale in 1967 and continued through 1968. The MK campaign, in which Chris Hani rose to prominence, had considerable propaganda value, but from a military point of view its successes were negligible. By the time of the Morogoro Conference held in Tanzania in 1969, MK had still not managed to fire a single shot within South Africa itself. This remained the case until after 1976.

The conspicuous lack of success in prosecuting the armed struggle featured prominently at the Morogoro Conference, as did the role of non-blacks within ANC structures. These two issues were in fact linked. Since 1962 the MK had assumed an increasingly important position within the ANC, as did the reconstituted Communist Party (SACP), which now redefined its core theory of 'colonialism of a special type' in the light of the new conditions. The 'national democratic revolution' remained its foremost objective as the first stage towards the achievement of socialism. But, whereas mass mobilisation was the preferred means to achieve the national revolution during the 1950s, political methods (including class politics) were henceforth subordinated to the imperatives of armed resistance. The examples of anti-colonial insurgency in Vietnam, China, Algeria, and especially Cuba, were cited in support of the theory that military activity could serve as the vanguard of revolution by inspiring popular uprisings within the country. Only gradually was it realised that dependence on military action was unrealistic and that the secretive nature of an externally based armed resistance movement compounded the ANC's difficulties in mobilising mass support within South Africa rather than assisting it. Thus, until the late 1970s, the primacy of the armed struggle over political activism remained a central tenet of ANC and SACP thinking. Even then, attitudes were slow to change. Throughout the 1980s, powerful elements within the ANC/SACP remained convinced that only a military-inspired 'seizure of power' could dislodge the apartheid regime.

A frequent justification of the military struggle was its value as 'armed propaganda'. But another possible explanation for the great importance accorded to the MK's military ambitions was its role in helping to cement the working relationship between the SACP and the ANC during the exile years. The SACP played a dominant role within MK and, through MK, the ANC itself. It was largely through the Party's intimate links with Moscow that the ANC was provided with vital material and military resources. The SACP also helped to sustain the ANC by providing it with organisational discipline, revolutionary theory and ideological certitude. Along with the SACP's contribution of intellectual and organisational muscle came its inculcation of authoritarian 'democratic-centralist' practices and attitudes. The close links between the ANC and the SACP are reflected in their pronouncements from the 1960s onwards, which were invariably framed in the leaden discourse of Marxist-Leninist revolutionary anti-imperialism. Such language made it easy for critics on the Left and, of course, the Right to allege that the ANC was little more than a communist front.

The reality was rather more complex. Within the uppermost echelons of revolutionary leadership, the relationship between the SACP and the ANC was so intimate that they were practically indistinguishable: many of the most talented members of the ANC were senior SACP cadres, even if, like Govan Mbeki's son, Thabo, they were not always orthodox Marxist-Leninists. However, the organisations retained their respective identities at lower levels, and the nationalist orientation of the ANC was never in question. Mutual dependence meant that the ANC/SACP alliance entailed reciprocal influences. The two-stage theory of revolution was the ideological embodiment of a political coalition built on pragmatic compromise. Crucially, the intricate nature of the ANC/SACP relationship meant that traditions of non-racism were sustained within the alliance without threatening the presumption of African leadership within the ANC proper. This delicate accommodation was formalised at the 1969 Morogoro Conference, which permitted members of 'minority groups' – whites, Coloureds and Indians – to join the external ANC (though they could not be members of the ANC national executive). On the other hand, membership of the newly constituted and highly influential Revolutionary Council was not restrictive, and here non-African SACP stalwarts like Yusuf Dadoo, Joe Slovo and Reg September played important roles. Dissent over white participation in the ANC surfaced periodically after Morogoro, and resulted in the expulsion of Tennyson Makiwane and seven other dissidents in 1975 for publicly declaring that the ANC had been hijacked by the communists at Morogoro. Nevertheless, the organisational framework adopted in 1969 mostly allowed such tensions to be contained.

EIGHT

A Revival in Internal Opposition

The early 1970s saw a gradual revival of political activity in South Africa, although the ANC played no direct role in this ferment until the second half of the decade. In 1973 a wave of spontaneous strikes involving over 60,000 workers erupted in Durban, which later spread to East London and the Witwatersrand. This labour militancy was a direct response to worsening economic conditions as the oil crisis precipitated an era of 'stagflation'. The strikes foreshadowed the growth of a dynamic union movement which, by the end of the decade, had come to constitute a powerful and permanent political force. Also based in Natal was Inkatha, a cultural and political movement revived by the Zulu nationalist leader, Chief Mangosuthu Buthelezi, in 1975. Buthelezi proved a masterful manipulator of Zulu ethnic sentiment, and skilfully used his equivocal position as a bantustan leader both to carve out a regional political base for himself and to attack the government upon whose patronage he depended. In the absence of legitimate domestic black opposition, Oliver Tambo offered Buthelezi considerable encouragement. Inkatha deliberately adopted the colours of the ANC, and Buthelezi often enunciated his support of Mandela. But the relationship soured from the end of the 1970s as Buthelezi adopted an increasingly conservative position and was denounced by the ANC as an apartheid 'puppet' and 'enemy of the people'.

The early 1970s also saw the emergence of the Black Consciousness (BC) movement, which defined liberation as a state of mind rather than in narrow political terms. Led by young student intellectuals like Steve Biko and radical Christian thinkers like Barney Pityana, BC focused on the need to counter internalised feelings of black inferiority with a determined sense of pride and self-assertion. The Black Consciousness movement had affinities with the Africanist Youth League and also with the PAC, but it was far more theoretically sophisticated than the Africanists, and differed from the Youth League in the sense that it existed independently of any single political organisation; unlike the PAC, BC defined 'black' in a manner that included Coloureds and Indians. Black Consciousness was inspired by a range of influences, including the Black Power movement in the United States, Senghor's philosophy of negritude, and the theories of racism and colonialism propounded by revolutionary intellectuals like Amilcar Cabral in Guinea-Bissau and Frantz Fanon in Algeria. The movement drew particular strength from the liberation of Mozambique and Angola which followed the collapse of the Portuguese African empire in 1974 (it was at this point that '*viva!*' became a popular cry in the South African political lexicon). Together with the heightened liberation struggle in Zimbabwe, these shifts in the balance of regional power underlined the growing vulnerability of white South Africa.

Black Consciousness had a palpable influence on the student-led Soweto uprisings of 1976–7, which were sparked off by spontaneous protests against the introduction of Afrikaans as a compulsory medium of instruction in black schools. The first student to die, Hector Petersen, was immortalised in a photograph which went round the world, showing his bloodied body being carried by friends. In the ensuing revolt which spread throughout South Africa, more than 600 mostly young people lost their lives. One of these was the pre-eminent Black Consciousness leader, Steve Biko, who was brutally killed while held in police detention in 1977. In his life and through his appalling death, Biko did more to transform perceptions of the South African political situation, both internally and externally, than any other single individual.

The Soweto uprising far exceeded the scale and intensity of the 1960 insurrection. It heralded the demise of white supremacy and made real the possibility of liberation, perhaps for the first time. Although the police eventually subdued the townships, the government would never again regain full control over the black population. White authority was no longer feared as it had been and 'the system' rather than the government was now the target of popular fury. An unquenchable spirit of rebellion was becoming manifest: the era of 'high apartheid' was at an end and the apartheid state was finally impelled to embark on an extensive programme of economic and social reforms.

Although the ANC had begun to rebuild an underground presence within the country, its role in the Soweto uprising was minimal. Student activists in the revolt later recorded that the ANC had barely figured in their political awareness. Nevertheless, the ANC was ideally placed to benefit from the dramatic events. Organisations affiliated to the Black Consciousness movement were systematically smashed after 1977, and as many as four to five thousand students, hardened by urban warfare and inspired by revolutionary enthusiasm, fled South Africa. In the neighbouring countries of Botswana, Swaziland, Lesotho and Zambia, many of these exiles were greeted by ANC operatives who directed them to MK training camps in Tanzania,

Angola and elsewhere. Had the PAC enjoyed a similar presence and infrastructure, it is possible that the Soweto generation would have strengthened its ranks. But the PAC had endured the exile years since 1960 far less well than the ANC, and now existed in little more than name.

The ANC's ideological outlook, political instincts and historical traditions were quite distinct from those of the Black Consciousness movement, and it was not attuned to the street-wise radicalism of the Soweto exiles. But it proved receptive to the energies of this youthful generation and showed sufficient flexibility to adapt to, and draw strength from, their revolutionary enthusiasms. The arrival on Robben Island of numbers of Black Consciousness activists provided a unique opportunity for the veteran ANC leadership to promote Charterist ideals and to inculcate theories of class struggle and organisational discipline. Many, though by no means all, BC leaders were gradually persuaded by the principles of non-racialism; in subsequent years they would explain (much to the annoyance of those who sought to keep BC traditions alive) that Black Consciousness was merely 'a phase' in the struggle for a non-racial socialist democracy. It was from the ranks of these post-Soweto and ex-Black Consciousness adherents that much of the impetus for 1980s-style community-based politics derived.

NINE

The Revolt of the 1980s

The ANC's ability to absorb a substantial proportion of the Black Consciousness movement was a vital aspect of its revival as a political force within South Africa during the 1980s. So, too, was its new-found capacity to launch a programme of sustained guerrilla activity. Spectacular acts of sabotage such as the bombing of the state's coal-to-oil installations in 1980, a rocket assault on the army headquarters in Pretoria in 1981, and an explosion at the country's only nuclear power station a year later, helped to confirm the ANC/SACP's dominant presence in the liberation struggle. In military terms, however, MK represented only a limited threat and its effectiveness declined after the signing of the 1984 Nkomati Accord which led to the removal of ANC bases from Mozambique.

A further indication of the ANC's determination to rebuild its constituency within the country were the concerted moves, from 1980, to reinstate the Freedom Charter as a living political document.

The launch of the 'Free Mandela' signature campaign – when Mandela was an ageing and almost forgotten prisoner – was an essential part of this process. So, too, was the re-emergence of the ANC's political iconography, songs and symbols at public events. To a remarkable extent, the character of mass politics during the 1980s consciously recalled Charterist traditions of the 1950s.

However, the 1980s were not the 1950s, and the domestic political landscape which the ANC confronted was infinitely more complex and crowded than it had been twenty years earlier. Perhaps the most striking development was the growth of a vigorous and mature labour movement. By the early 1980s a number of powerful union federations, as well as individual unions, were in existence. For the purposes of simplicity, and to use the categories of the day, it makes sense to distinguish between 'workerist' unions, which laid particular stress on workplace issues, internal democracy and working-class leadership, and 'populist' unions, which adopted an overtly political stance and, taking a lead from the experience of SACTU in the 1950s, sought to integrate worker power within local community and wider nationalist struggles. Workerist and (especially) populist unions were both inclined to the non-racial traditions of the Congress Alliance, although the influence of Marxist trade union theory on the former meant they were reluctant to become mere affiliates of the 'bourgeois' ANC – as SACTU was alleged to have become. Ranged against them were unions disposed to Black Consciousness and Africanist ideologies. These found common cause in their opposition to the involvement of whites in leadership positions. In 1985 unions sympathetic to the Congress movement came together to form the Congress of South African Trade Unions (Cosatu). A year later a smaller but significant rival federation loyal to Black Consciousness traditions was constituted as the National Council of Trade Unions. Total union membership at this time was about 1.5 million.

A second important development was the countrywide growth of community or civic organisations. These popular democratic groupings campaigned on issues like education, housing, rents and consumer issues, and included youth groups, sports clubs and religious associations. Hundreds of such civic organisations were drawn together to form the United Democratic Front, whose launch in 1983 represented a daring test of the government's preparedness to tolerate extra-parliamentary political opposition. At its peak the UDF had an affiliated membership of more than two million and claimed the support of many more. The heterodox social composition and political orientation of the UDF involved an alliance of races, classes and

86

generations. Unlike the ANC, which had become highly secretive and hierarchical in its years of exile, the UDF professed an open and democratic style of mass politics. But although very much an indigenous product of the distinctive popular radicalism of the 1980s, the UDF sought inspiration and legitimacy in Congress traditions of the 1950s. The Freedom Charter was now dusted down and relaunched as a popular manifesto – accompanied by vigorous debates as to whether its principles implied a socialist or social democratic future. Leaders and patrons of the UDF included veterans of ANC and BC politics as well as young political activists. The ANC underground was influential in its formation, but the UDF was in no simple sense a 'front' for the ANC – as the state frequently charged. Its emergence can only be understood in terms of the intricate dynamics of post-1976 internal politics, though it owed a natural allegiance to the ANC and its formation did much to facilitate Congress's re-entry into the sphere of open public politics.

The proximate reason for the UDF's creation, and the rallying causes around which it developed, were the need to fight government proposals for a new constitutional dispensation as well as tough new legislation designed to regulate the freedoms of African city-dwellers. Aiming to co-opt Coloureds and Indians into the political process – while simultaneously reaffirming the exclusion of Africans – the new constitution marked the culmination of a wide-ranging set of reforms inaugurated after the 1976 uprising. In 1978 the incoming prime minister, P.W. Botha, had famously asserted that apartheid had to 'adapt or die'. The institutional reforms which followed this pronouncement were in part a response to a struggling economy that was increasingly hamstrung by the structural inefficiencies of the late apartheid system. They were also a consequence of the state's belated realisation of the need to construct a stable black middle class as a social buffer against popular radicalism. Among the most important reforms introduced in the post-1977 period were those which led to official recognition of black trade unions, increased resources for black education, provided greater security and improved amenities for Africans with urban 'insider' rights, introduced changes in local government administration, and helped to forge closer ties between big business and the state.

The government reforms were not merely cosmetic or 'irrelevant', as some opponents charged, but nor were they motivated by a genuine desire to end apartheid. On the contrary, Botha sought to preserve the underlying basis of white supremacy by stripping away the more odious aspects of apartheid in an attempt to broaden the political and social foundations upon which the system of racial capitalism rested. Reforms were accompanied by a greatly enhanced role for the military in domestic politics and a conspicuous retreat away from Verwoerdian ideological nostrums. Apartheid's defence was instead couched in terms of a moral and military crusade against communism. The government hoped that authoritarian reform initiated from above would subvert revolution from below. But the reforms initiated by Botha's technocrats never succeeded in gaining wider political legitimacy, and political concessions only served to encourage demands for further change.

It has often been observed that the stability of a repressive regime is most at risk when it embarks upon reform and that its position is made even more precarious when it attempts to halt the process. This was powerfully borne out in the mid-1980s. The spark of revolt came in 1984, when rent increases were announced in the industrial regions of the Transvaal. The increases were imposed by a new tier of frequently corrupt black local councillors (empowered by local government reforms) who were commonly viewed as apartheid functionaries. Such 'collaborators' were an obvious and accessible target of hate for ordinary township residents. In September, matters came to a head when violent confrontations led to the occupation of townships in the Transvaal by police and army units. But instead of succeeding in restoring order, as had happened after 1960 and 1976, the struggle was intensified and the 'Vaal uprising' soon spread to the Eastern Cape, Orange Free State and Natal. After 1985 the revolt extended to the notionally independent and self-governing black homelands (or bantustans) where corruption and clientilism had reached intolerable proportions. From 1985 to 1986 there were well over 2,000 deaths as a result of political violence. Tens of thousands of activists were detained or went into hiding. Of the countless incidents that might be mentioned, one stands out in particular: the unprovoked killing by police of more than twenty unarmed mourners in a funeral procession – on the 25th anniversary of the 1960 Sharpeville massacre.

In July 1985 a state of emergency was declared over large parts of South Africa – the first since Sharpeville. A massive crackdown by the security forces ensued in which thousands of activists were arrested. Many were tortured, some were killed. But the violence was not quelled. In August, P.W. Botha delivered his heavily trailed 'Rubicon' address, which was televised live throughout the world. Instead of introducing further reforms, as had been widely presumed, he defied local and international opinion and indignantly warned the outside world not to 'push us too far'. International investors took fright and refused to renew loans to the government, the South African currency collapsed, and a moratorium on payments of foreign debt was imposed. The political crisis deepened dramatically and in June 1986, after a brief respite, a second even more severe state of emergency was imposed which lasted until the end of 1990.

In magnitude, intensity and form, the 1984–6 popular rebellion represented an unprecedented explosion of violence and repression. It is impossible to describe the wave of unrest in any detail, but two points should be noted: first, the conflict was only partially conducted along racial lines because the infrastructure of the apartheid system – in local government, the bantustans and the army – was composed of an increasingly high proportion of blacks; second, although the environment in which conflict took place was deeply politicised and involved broad party affiliations, the direction of events was controlled and co-ordinated only to a limited extent by political parties or movements. Even if it wished to claim credit for the unrest, the ANC was not the orchestrator of revolt. When, in January 1985, Oliver Tambo broadcast an instruction on behalf of the ANC to 'render South Africa ungovernable' he was describing an already existing state of affairs rather than prescribing a course of action.

The pattern of violence and repression took various forms. Often led by township 'youth' or 'comrades' (a broad category which included students, radical activists and thugs), there were frequent attacks on 'sell-out' township police and councillors. Boycotts of white businesses and stay-aways from school and places of work were frequently called, and brutally enforced. The popular cry of 'liberation before education' signalled the effective collapse of formal schooling and the rise of a generation whose anger could no longer be contained by force. The police and army attempted to quell opposition through indiscriminate use of tear-gas, rubber bullets and, sometimes, live ammunition. They also conducted waves of arrests and detentions in which the torture of activists figured prominently. Assassinations of prominent political figures were common. Such terror tactics were abetted by local vigilantes, militia and warlords, who were either sponsored by the state or else operated with the connivance of the security forces. Mass political funerals and rallies often occasioned further violence, either in response to police provocation, or as *impimpis* (collaborators) were pointed out by the crowd. The most gruesome form of killing was 'necklacing': placing a burning tyre filled with petrol round the neck of a supposed enemy of the struggle. This practice was notoriously supported by Winnie Mandela, the then wife of Nelson, who told a mass rally in 1986 that the oppressed masses would liberate the country 'with necklaces and our little boxes of matches'.

In broad terms the violence was conducted between those who proclaimed themselves to be UDF or Cosatu supporters on the one hand and agents of the state on the other. From 1985, however, the conflict took on a new, apparently ethnic, and even more murderous dimension. Buthelezi's Inkatha movement became embroiled in a conflict with Zulu-speaking supporters of the UDF and Cosatu in Natal. The internecine struggle verged on becoming a regional civil war as villagers and urban township-dwellers fought each other in a merciless cycle of revenge attacks of which the Pietermaritzburg area was the epicentre. In 1990 the violence spilt over to the townships of the Witwatersrand when Zulu migrant workers clashed with ANC-supporting comrades. By this time the conflict had claimed around four thousand lives. Thousands more ordinary people were to die before the 1994 election.

The origins of the conflict and the responsibility for the violence remain highly contentious. Right-wingers, both in South Africa and overseas, commended Buthelezi as a political moderate and a supporter of free enterprise with whom they could work. Cynics took comfort in the notion that mindless 'black on black' or 'tribal' violence was an innate aspect of the African condition. The government – whose shadowy 'Third Force' secretly armed and trained Inkatha – portrayed the 'tribal' conflict as a reason for denying black majority rule.

Conversely, politicians and academics with left-wing sympathies demonised Buthelezi, charged Inkatha as the principal aggressor, and sought to demonstrate that Buthelezi's manipulation of Zulu identity, coupled with profound socio-economic divisions, were the root causes of the crisis. Such arguments only served to fuel the conflict, and considerably undermined the ANC's central claim to represent all South Africans regardless of ethnic and racial origin.

TEN

Negotiations

By 1988 the struggle for South Africa was in a state of murderous and intractable stalemate. The forces of opposition had proved unable to defeat an apartheid state whose lethal powers were undiminished and still extended within and beyond the country's borders. The government had succeeded in consolidating its position among white South Africans at the 1987 general election when the white electorate moved sharply to the Right. At the time Mandela reflected that the National Party had never been stronger. But the Botha regime, though seemingly gaining the upper hand in the struggle to contain endemic revolt, was not able to re-establish its authority over black South Africa. The popularity of the ANC and the Communist Party in the black townships was higher than ever before; unsurprisingly, the government's greatest declared enemy was embraced as a staunch ally of liberation.

The government's grip was being steadily eroded by a fast-deteriorating economic situation which was aggravated by the imposition of international sanctions and a loss of business confidence. But its capacity to wreak havoc was undiminished. Calculated destabilisation by the military of the Marxist-supporting governments of Mozambique and Angola engulfed these countries in civil war, and South Africa's 'securocrats', now virtually unrestrained by civil powers, attacked ANC targets beyond South Africa's borders at will. For its part, MK had finally established secure supply routes and infiltrated several hundred trained operatives organized in cells throughout the country. By the late 1980s bombs, shootings and explosions were daily occurrences. MK's hope of leading a full-scale 'people's war' was, however, still far off. Those who had blithely said the choice for the future was between violent revolution and peaceful evolution were confronted with the reality of violent evolution at best and, at worst, descent into an abyss of uncontained chaos.

Internationally, South Africa was becoming a major focus of attention and concern. By the mid-1980s, Johannesburg was regarded as one of the top international postings for a foreign journalist – and undoubtedly the most exciting. Tightening military, trade, cultural and sporting sanctions proved highly demoralising for white South Africans, in addition to being economically costly. With the South African military engaged in waging war on neighbouring countries, the government's standard response to overseas criticism – that its sovereignty and internal affairs should be respected – lacked credibility. The domestic image of South Africa's invincibility was seriously dented when, in 1988, the South African Army faced defeat by Cuban troops supporting Angolan government forces at Cuito-Cuanavale. This event proved a turning point in military and strategic thinking. A direct consequence was the government's decision to finally end South Africa's illegal occupation of Namibia from 1989, on condition that Cuba withdraw its armed presence from Angola. White South African power in the region was undeniably being rolled back; in addition, an important precedent for negotiated political transition was thereby established.

Behind the scenes pragmatists, realists – and even some idealists – were seeking a breakthrough. Tentative dialogue between Mandela and the Botha government had been established in 1985 through a semi-private initiative of the Justice Minister. In 1986 contact was secretly made in New York between the leader of the secretive Afrikaner Broederbond and Tambo's increasingly influential adviser, Thabo Mbeki, one of the few senior ANC figures who favoured talks with the government at this stage. Meetings with the ANC were also arranged between business leaders, Afrikaner academics and opinion-formers, most dramatically in Dakar in 1987. Care had to be taken that these meetings did not commit either side to any position; they were invariably informal and unofficial. At such gatherings curiosity soon got the better of mutual suspicion, though the great bogey of 'communism' remained a major stalling point for most whites. Whites' fears of wholesale property expropriation and godless communism were, however, allayed through personal contacts, reassurances, and a general air of reasonableness. Alcohol-fuelled meetings in congenial locations did much to lift veils of prejudice, while nostalgia and sentiment often facilitated mutual recognition of a common sense of South Africanness. A spirit of conciliation was being born as two formidable adversaries faced up to each other.

From the mid-1980s audiences with the ANC were increasingly sought by Western governments in recognition of the evident fact that the ANC would have to be a participant in any credible political settlement. The virulent hostility expressed towards the ANC by Margaret Thatcher and Ronald Reagan was thus increasingly countermanded by their governments' own intelligence services and diplomatic officials, who were realising that rival organisations like Inkatha or the PAC were unlikely post-apartheid victors. Foreign perceptions of the South African conflict were significantly affected by the visit to South Africa in May 1986 of a team of

Commonwealth 'eminent persons' whose peace-
making efforts were sabotaged when the South
African military launched a series of raids on alleged
ANC bases in the surrounding Commonwealth
countries of Zambia, Zimbabwe and Botswana. This
deliberate act of provocation and defiance did much
to harden Western opinion against the Botha regime
and, reciprocally, to strengthen the hand of the ANC.

High-profile meetings between Tambo and senior
representatives of the British and United States
governments in 1986 and 1987 also served to
enhance the ANC's international diplomatic status.
Indeed, the exiled ANC now enjoyed more
extensive and much warmer overseas recognition
than the official South African government.
Substantial material and ideological support from
Scandinavian countries, Sweden in particular,
helped to break the ANC's dependence on the
Soviet bloc. Public opinion in the United States and
Britain was notably in advance of their right-wing
Cold War warrior leaders. The American and British
liberal-left opposition, frustrated by the ideological
hegemony of Thatcherism and Reaganism, elevated
the South African struggle to the status of an
international moral cause from the early 1980s and
campaigned for tougher economic sanctions,
targeting multinational businesses like Barclays
Bank in particular. The ANC was undoubtedly the
greatest beneficiary of international solidarity and

boycott movements at this time. Mandela began to attain iconic status. The global world of pop music and youth culture turned him into a martyr of world freedom, most dramatically at a 1988 Wembley rock concert organised to celebrate his seventieth birthday.

By 1988 the South African situation was widely perceived to be critical and worsening. Only the most optimistic observers and participants in the struggle forecast a positive short-term future. An international discussion group of leading scholars convened by Lord Bullock reached consensus on one issue: 'the auguries for a "negotiated settlement" – which we understood to mean a substantive reallocation of political power in favour of the representative leaders of the black majority – are poor.' (S. Johnson (ed.), *South Africa: No Turning Back* (Indiana, 1989), p. 375). The deadlock was broken by a series of important and dramatic developments the following year. In the Harare Declaration of August 1989 the ANC set out terms under which it was prepared to enter into negotiations with the government. In September, F.W. de Klerk succeeded P.W. Botha, the 'Great Crocodile', as South African president. And in October the Berlin Wall was breached as Eastern European Communist politicians were swept from power. De Klerk's rise did not immediately signal major change because his reputation was as a conservative party *apparatchik* rather than a vigorous or idealistic reformer. But it did at least mean that the intransigent, bitter and enfeebled Botha – who had by now come to represent the greatest single political barrier to change – was finally removed from power. For its part, the fall of communism removed the single most important ideological constraint on change: no longer could the government assert that control over southern Africa represented the Kremlin's greatest prize.

De Klerk did not anticipate ending the system which had brought him to power, nor did he undergo a sudden political conversion. Like Gorbachev, he hoped instead to regain the political initiative by wrong-footing his enemies. This de Klerk did in spectacular fashion on the occasion of the opening of parliament on 2 February 1990. The new president astonished even his closest colleagues by announcing the unbanning of the ANC, PAC and SACP, and the imminent release of hundreds of political prisoners, including Nelson Mandela. Notwithstanding the mood of intense expectancy in early 1990, de Klerk had gone further than anyone had anticipated by opening up the political process without preconditions. Nine days later, Mandela was free.

Conclusion

It took another four years for the country's first fully democratic elections to be held and for Mandela to be elected president of South Africa with over 60 per cent of the popular vote. The transition from white supremacy to multiracial democracy in what has come to be known as the 'miracle' of South Africa's 'negotiated revolution' has yet to be studied in historical depth. In any case, a full account of how this protracted and contorted process came to pass is beyond the scope of this short history. Suffice it to say that the path was fraught with dangers and frequently bloody. In 1990 alone there were 3,700 political fatalities. Within this unstable political environment ground rules had to be established, constitutional guidelines laid down, political parties formed, constituencies wooed and realigned. For the ANC, the task of transforming itself from a liberation movement into a political party with a coherent organisational structure was a particular challenge.

The Convention for a Democratic South Africa (Codesa), which oversaw the overall process of transition, first met at the end of 1991. Over two hundred delegates representing nineteen political parties were there, though the PAC was absent at the start and Inkatha withdrew six months later. Structured negotiations collapsed in June 1992 following a massacre of forty-five shack-dwellers at Boipatong for which Inkatha and agents of the state were generally blamed. In order to consolidate its power base and to exert direct political pressure on the government, the ANC now unleashed a campaign of 'rolling mass action'; this culminated in a massive general strike and the killing of twenty-eight ANC demonstrators at Bisho in the Ciskei. The rapidly deteriorating situation prompted Mandela and de Klerk to sign a landmark Record of Understanding in September 1992 which brought the ANC and the government together in a bilateral relationship and, crucially, began to limit Inkatha's scope to instigate political violence. In March 1993 formal negotiations were resumed within the framework of a Multi-Party Negotiating Forum, and in November agreement was finally reached on an interim constitution. A Transitional Executive Council was created to oversee the process of transfer of power and to supervise the holding of national elections. An interim ANC/National Party government had, in effect, been formed.

Two factors in particular played a part in the drawn-out interregnum: first, the government's determination to prolong the transition process as much as possible in the hope of expanding its own support base and inducing splits within the ANC; second, its insistence on complex constitutional and procedural arrangements to secure 'power sharing', 'group rights', federalism and a diminished role for the central state. But de Klerk had miscalculated. The longer the negotiation process was extended, the more power began to leach away from the government into the hands of the ascendant ANC. The government's dodges and delaying tactics should not, however, be seen in terms of cool political calculus alone, for it was also part of a deeper process of psychological acclimatisation: the National Party, continuously in government from 1948 and prime upholder of apartheid, was engaged in an extraordinary process of talking itself out of power.

Although the outcome of negotiations could not be forecast in 1990, it was soon apparent that the government and the ANC were the principal negotiating parties. The leading negotiators, Cyril Ramaphosa, ANC Secretary-General, and Roelf Meyer, Deputy Minister of Constitutional Development, formed a strong personal understanding, and they remained closely in touch even when negotiations were formally suspended. Many other figures played vital facilitating roles. But although individual contributions were crucial, the impulse to come to a working accord lay deeper. By 1991 it was clear that no accord was possible without the agreement of the ANC and the National Party. Recognition of this fact by each of these parties implied an acceptance that neither could withdraw from the process without threatening its own primacy as a negotiating partner – let alone a peaceful outcome for the country. Almost from the start of negotiations the ANC and the National Party were therefore inexorably locked together on an uncertain journey from which there could in reality be no turning back. Yet, until the eve of the election it was entirely possible that Inkatha-led violence or a military coup might stall or reverse the entire process and lead to complete social and political breakdown.

Fears of unstoppable chaos fed a 'normalising' counter-current which meant that the extraordinary ANC-National Party embrace became a matter of almost ordinary political reality. Yet it should be remembered how unlikely this outcome would have seemed just a few years earlier, let alone when viewed in longer perspective: that the ANC and the National Party could see themselves striking a deal before 1990 was implausible; in 1988 it would have seemed wildly optimistic; in 1980 barely conceivable; in 1960 all indications were that the ANC had been crushed by the Nationalists; in 1912, when the ANC and the National Party were both in the process of being created, the prospect of their working together to create a 'new' South Africa would not even have been a meaningful proposition. The fact that the ANC, in alliance with the Communist Party and Cosatu, formed a Government of National Unity with the National Party in 1994 was thus a remarkable, and in many ways surprising, resolution of the struggle for popular democracy in South Africa.

Writing of the twentieth-century triumph of democracy in Europe in his book *Dark Continent: Europe's Twentieth Century* (Harmondsworth, 1998), Mark Mazower has described 'a story of narrow squeaks and unexpected twists, not inevitable victories and forward marches', (p. xii). He might just as easily have been thinking of the ANC and South Africa. There are many contingent factors as well as structural forces which have to be taken into account in explaining, firstly, the ANC's victory, and secondly, its character as a governing party. Had the ANC come to power before the end of the Soviet empire, it is likely that the influence upon it of the Communist Party and Cosatu would have predominated over the nationalist and social democratic-inclined party that eventually took office. The story of how the 'exiled' ANC gained ascendancy over the internal movement, why the UDF chose to go into voluntary liquidation in 1991 and what the implications of this decision have been for the making of a non-racial democracy has yet to be fully traced or explored. Also perplexing, notwithstanding its well-documented history of internal divisions and organisational collapse, was the disappearance of the PAC as a credible political party and the declining influence of radical Black Consciousness organisations such as the National Council of Trade Unions and the Azanian People's Organisation. The rapprochement between Inkatha and the ANC in the late 1990s has been another unlikely development (which raises serious questions as to whether the murderous conflict between them was avoidable). And the slow but visible fragmenting of the triple alliance between the ANC, Cosatu and the SACP in the period since 1994 is indicative of the problems and new realities faced by a liberation movement turned governing party.

What, then, secured the pre-eminence of the ANC and allowed it to consolidate its position in the run-up to the 1994 election? Aside from the many circumstantial factors which favoured the ANC, three underlying structural tendencies should be mentioned. In the first place, moderation and inclusivity: for most of its history, the ANC's traditions of non-sectarian, broad-church politics meant that its leaders were predisposed to seek the political middle ground. This meant that the ANC was generally able to absorb radical forces of opposition to white supremacy, such as militant Africanist and class-based politics, without these impulses displacing the power and authority of the moderate centre. Although the ANC suffered on occasion from weak or indecisive leadership, at no time in its history (with the sole possible exception of Gumede's brief tenure) was it led by a radical. As a corollary, it may also be worth noting that despite the ANC's overt hostility towards bourgeois liberal politics and ideology during its years of exile, long-standing liberal and social democratic orientations and traditions were never entirely expunged from the organisation or its nationalist-minded leadership; indeed, the 1990s has seen the re-emergence of the ANC as a social democratic-inclined party to an extent that would have been inconceivable a decade before.

Second, longevity and survival: as the oldest and most consistent African resistance movement the ANC succeeded in accumulating enormous reserves of symbolic capital. The public memory of the ANC was powerful enough to sustain the organisation through lean times, and always provided opportunities for its rehabilitation. Generational conflict was an important component of the struggle, but respect for seniority, experience and loyalty remained strong. The perseverance and resilience of the ANC, and of the Youth League veterans in particular, was widely admired. Political survival in the uncongenial circumstances of three decades of exile was in itself an achievement which conferred authority and legitimacy on the organisation.

Third, a broad front: supporters of the ANC spanned a greater range of social groups and ideological positions than any other competing party or organisation. In partnership with the SACP and Cosatu, the ANC was the leading element in a tripartite alliance which encompassed long-standing traditions of non-racialism, African nationalism and socialism. The ANC was also structured as an alliance – a cumbersome organisational arrangement which ultimately proved advantageous. Three distinct elements were involved in this coalition: an external mission based in Europe and Africa incorporating political and military wings; an internal movement grouped around the UDF and Cosatu, and finally, the Robben Island prison diaspora.

Each of these elements made a distinct contribution to the ANC's eventual success. Following the crippling reverses of the 1960s and early 1970s, the ANC's external and internal wings had succeeded by the 1980s in establishing it as the most credible inheritor of political power in any future dispensation. This was an essential precondition of the ANC's rise to political pre-eminence. What proved decisive, however, was the unimpeachable moral authority that attached to the Robben Islanders and other exiled members of the early 'struggle' generation. This leadership-in-limbo, which had mostly come to prominence in the 1950s, possessed a prestige and seniority that few internal leaders were able to boast. Their credentials in the struggle were indisputable, and yet they also remained unsullied by direct involvement in recent politics.

In sum, we might conclude that the combination of the ANC's long history, the breadth of its social and ideological span, its presence in as *well* as its absence from the bitter struggles of the 1980s all help to explain why it was best placed to accede to power when the long-awaited moment of liberation finally arrived. In a struggle which lasted for most of the twentieth century the continent's first major African nationalist movement had survived to lead the last African country to political freedom.

Further Reading

Any serious account of the history of the ANC, however selective, must begin with Peter Walshe's now dated but still classic account of the period up to 1952, *The Rise of African Nationalism in South Africa* (London, 1970). Tom Lodge's *Black Politics in South Africa Since 1945* (Johannesburg, 1983), which takes the story up to 1976, combines the sharp insights of a political scientist with a distinctive social history approach and remains the most reliable and influential account of postwar resistance politics. Gail Gerhart's *Black Power in South Africa* (California University Press, Berkeley and Los Angeles, 1978) treats the history of black resistance from a more Africanist point of view, concentrating on the Pan-Africanist Congress and the Black Consciousness movement. Unmatched as a resource for teaching and writing is the five-volume documentary history of African politics produced by Thomas Karis, Gwendolen Carter, Gail Gerhart and Sheridan Johns, *From Protest to Challenge* (Stanford, Bloomington and Cambridge, Mass., 1972–97). This massive contribution combines invaluable archival material with judicious interpretive overviews and biographical profiles. For Thomas Karis in particular it represents the labour of more than thirty-five years.

Francis Meli's *South Africa Belongs to Us* (Harare, 1988) is the closest one gets to an official internal history of the ANC. Jack and Ray Simons' influential *Class and Colour in South Africa 1850–1950* (Harmondsworth, 1969) is an important work by scholar-activists with a lifetime commitment to the ANC and the Communist Party. Mary Benson's *South Africa: The Struggle for a Birthright* (Harmondsworth, 1966) is an elegantly written overview by a sympathetic insider and observer. Ranged against these insider accounts are the critical assessments of B. Hirson, *Yours for the Union: Class and Community Struggles in South Africa 1930–47* (London, 1990); D.T. McKinley, *The ANC and the Liberation Struggle* (1997); S. Ellis and T. Sechaba, *Comrades Against Apartheid: The ANC and the South African Communist Party in Exile* (London, 1992) and Howard Barrell's *MK: The ANC's Armed Struggle* (Harmondsworth, 1990).

Among the more important accounts of resistance politics from the 1980s are those by Tom Lodge and Bill Nasson, *All Here and Now: Black Politics in South Africa in the 1980s* (London, 1992), Martin Murray, *South Africa: Time of Agony, Time of Destiny* (London, 1987), W. Cobbett and R. Cohen (eds), *Popular Struggles in South Africa* (London, 1988), N. Etherington (ed.), *Peace, Politics and Violence in the New South Africa* (London, 1992) and S. Johnson (ed.), *South Africa: No Turning Back* (Basingstoke, 1988). The *Journal of Southern African Studies* special issue on the 'Social History of Resistance in South Africa' vol. 18, no. 2 (1992) contains a number of important contributions by younger scholars.

A full and authoritative history of the negotiations process and the transition to majority rule has yet to be written, but the most useful so far include those by journalists: A. Sparks, *Tomorrow is Another Country* (London, 1995), S. Friedman (ed.) *The Long Journey: South Africa's Quest for a Negotiated Settlement* (Johannesburg, 1993) and P. Waldmeir, *Anatomy of a Miracle* (New York, 1997). H. Adam and K. Moodley's *The Opening of the Apartheid Mind* (Berkeley, 1993) and H. Adam et al: *Comrades in Business* (Cape Town, 1997) offer valuable sociological perspectives. Discussons by liberals unsympathetic to the ANC include H. Giliomee et al: *The Bold Experiment: South Africa's New Democracy* (Halfway House, 1994) and R.W. Johnson and L.

Schlemmer (eds), *Launching Democracy: South Africa's First Open Election* (Yale, 1996).

Political biographies and autobiographies are a rapidly growing genre in South Africa and provide essential insights into the lives and thinking of key individuals. Some of the most important examples include Nelson Mandela's *Long Walk to Freedom* (London, 1994), Albert Luthuli's *Let My People Go* (London, 1962), S Biko's *I Write What I Like* (London, 1978), A. Sampson's *Mandela* (London, 1999), M Gevisser's forthcoming biography of Thabo Mbeki, and B. Pogrund's *How Can Man Die Better . . . Sobukwe and Apartheid* (London, 1990).

Academic interpretations of South African society and history provide a broader context and analytical structure within which to interpret the rise of the ANC. Good overviews include W. Beinart, *Twentieth-Century South Africa* (Oxford, 1994), N. Worden, *The Making of Modern South Africa* (Oxford, 1994), R. Ross, *A Concise History of South Africa* (Cambridge, 1999) and the *Reader's Digest Illustrated History of South Africa* (Cape Town, 1988). More specialised, and reflective of the influential social history tradition in South African historiography, is P. Bonner et.al. (eds), *Apartheid's Genesis 1935–1962* (Johannesburg, 1993) and B. Bozzoli (ed.), *Class Community and Conflict: South African Perspectives* (Johannesburg, 1987). S. Marks and S. Trapido (eds), *The Politics of Class, Race and Nationalism in Twentieth-Century South Africa* (Harlow, 1987) and W. Beinart and S. Dubow (eds), *Segregation and Apartheid in Twentieth-Century South Africa* (London, 1995) are collections of influential scholarly work on modern South African history and politics. Both carry substantial introductions by the editors.

113

Index

African Claims 23–4, 33
African People's Organisation 2, 37, 52
Africanist 11–12, 15–17, 27–33, 39, 51, 57–8, 59–61, 80, 86, 107, 111
All-African Convention 18–19
ANC: Congress Alliance 37–8, 39, 40, 52–3, 56; Independent ANC 16; SANNC (South African Native National Congress) 1–7, 8–9; Youth League 27–33, 36, 57, 108; and *passim*
apartheid 35, 40, 71–2, 82, 88–9, 91
armed struggle: MK 66, 68, 69, 74–7, 84, 96

Biko, Steve 80, 81
Black Consciousness 80–3, 84, 107
Botha, P.W. 88–9, 90, 95, 97, 99, 100–1
boycotts and strikes 35–6, 47, 79, 92, 103
Buthelezi, Mangosuthu 79–80, 93–4

Christianity 4, 8–9, 16, 43
Codesa 102–3
Communism 12–14, 31–3, 37, 39, 53–4, 65, 72–3, 75–8, 98, 101, 106, 107, 109

Defiance Campaign 39–45
de Klerk, F.W. 100–1, 103–4
Dube, John 3, 16

Fischer, Bram 69
Franchise Action Council 38
Freedom Charter 51–2, 56, 57–8, 84, 87

Gandhi, Mahatma 37
Garvey, Marcus 11, 15
Gumede, Josiah 13, 16, 107–8

Harare Declaration 100
Hertzog, J.B.M. 12–13, 16–19 *passim*

Industrial and Commercial Workers' Union vi, 12
Inkatha 79–80, 93–4, 103, 105, 107
international response 44, 60, 62–3, 64, 73, 90–1, 95–7, 98–100

Jabavu, D.D.T. 18–19

Kgosana, Philip 63

Leballo, Potlako 59, 60, 62, 70
legislation 5–6, 8, 10, 17–19, 31, 35, 38–9, 40, 47, 50, 61–3, 68
Lembede, Anton 27, 28–30
Liberal Party 63, 65, 67
liberals 51, 58, 65, 112
Luthuli, Albert 43, 49, 67

M-plan 50, 65
Malan, D.F. 21, 30, 35, 40–1
Mandela, Nelson: in Youth League 27, 28, 30, 32–3; activist 50, 65, 66; in prison 68–70, 73–4, 85, 97, 100; release and after xii–xiii, 101, 102, 103
Mandela, Winnie 92
Mbeki, Govan 19, 48–9, 70
Mbeki, Thabo 77, 97
Mda, Peter 27, 29
Meyer, Roelf 104
Moroka, Dr James 28, 31, 36, 43, 45
Mpanza, James 25

Natal Indian Congress 2, 32
National Party 12–13, 21, 95, 104, 105
Ndobe, Bransby 14–15, 16
'necklacing' 92
Ngubane, Jordan 30, 32–3

PAC (Pan African Congress) 59–65, 66, 83, 101, 103, 107; *see also* Africanist
Petersen, Hector 81

Plaatje, Solomon 3, 5–6
Pondoland Revolt 64
Programme of Action 33, 34–5, 57, 60

Ramaphosa, Cyril 104
Rand Revolt 12
resistance v, x, 9, 10, 11, 16, 25, 27, 31, 37, 43, 47, 49, 63, 64, 76, 108
Rivonia trial 68–70
Robben Island xiii, 70, 73–4, 83, 109

Seme, Pixley 3, 16, 19, 28
Sharpeville 46, 62–3, 64
Sisulu, Walter 27, 28, 30, 70, 74
Smuts, Jan 12, 21, 22, 26
Sobukwe, Robert 59–60, 62, 70
Sophiatown 46–7
South Africa: dominion 1–2, 5, 9–10, 13; republic 65, 67–8, 71, 87–8, 95–101; democracy 102–6
Soweto uprisings 81–2
squatters 21, 25

Tambo, Oliver 28, 30, 64, 70, 72, 80, 91, 99
Tonjeni, Elliot 14–15, 16
trades union movement 10, 11–12, 22, 25–6, 37, 53, 79, 85–6, 93, 106, 109
Treason Trial 52, 56–7, 68

UDF (United Democratic Front) 86–7, 93, 106
United Nations 44, 62–3, 73

Verwoerd, Hendrik 67, 71

women 6, 47, 52–3, 54–6

Xuma, Dr Alfred B. 20, 24–32 *passim*

Youth League 27–33, 36, 57, 108; *see also* African National Congress